The
Historical Directory of Sussex County, New Jersey

CONTAINING
A BRIEF SUMMARY OF EVENTS FROM ITS FIRST SETTLEMENT,
WITH DESCRIPTIVE AND HISTORICAL NOTICES OF EACH TOWN

ALSO

THE NAME AND POST OFFICE ADDRESS OF EACH FREEHOLDER

EMBELLISHED WITH ILLUSTRATION
AND
A VALUABLE MAP OF THE COUNTY

Compiled and Edited by
Edward A. Webb

HERITAGE BOOKS
2007

HERITAGE BOOKS
AN IMPRINT OF HERITAGE BOOKS, INC.

Books, CDs, and more—Worldwide

For our listing of thousands of titles see our website
at
www.HeritageBooks.com

A Facsimile Reprint
Published 2007 by
HERITAGE BOOKS, INC.
Publishing Division
65 East Main Street
Westminster, Maryland 21157-5026

Originally published
1872

— Publisher's Notice —
In reprints such as this, it is often not possible to remove blemishes from the original. We feel the contents of this book warrant its reissue despite these blemishes and hope you will agree and read it with pleasure.

International Standard Book Number: 978-1-55613-672-6

INTRODUCTION.

THE historical and descriptive notices of Sussex County, and its towns, which are brought together in this volume, have been gleaned from many sources, and by various means.

By minute personal observation in frequent visits made to all the places described.

By free conversations with a large number of the most intelligent and trustworthy of the citizens.

By valuable manuscripts prepared by residents familiar with the unwritten history of their own neighborhood.

The compiler has made very free use of a number of works from which he has quoted largely and literally, among which he would enumerate "Messrs. Edsall's and Tuttle's Centennial Addresses;" quotations from Mr. Edsall's Essay are more numerous than from all other sources.

"Eager's History of Orange County," "Barber's History of New Jersey," "History and Characteristics of the Reformed Dutch Church," "Historical Sermon" by the Rev. P. Kanouse, and "Sypher's History of New Jersey," have been consulted and used in this compilation.

Especial mention is gratefully made of Mr. T. G. Bunnell, editor and proprietor of the "New Jersey Herald," in Newton, to whom the compiler is indebted for much valuable material, kindly and freely furnished.

ANDOVER, September, 1872.

Historical Sketch of the County.

THAT part of the State of New Jersey now known as Sussex County was first explored and settled by the Dutch on the 11th of September, 1609, the Half Moon, a vessel of eighty tons burden, commanded by Hendrick Hudson, passed through the Narrows and anchored in New York harbor. Hudson came under the auspices of the Dutch East India Company to seek for a north-west passage to the East Indies. With this purpose he sailed up to where Albany is now situated. There he found that he could proceed no farther. Other vessels were subsequently sent out by the Company, and trading posts were established both at Albany (which they then called Fort Orange) and on the Island of Manhattan (now New York). This was in the year 1614, six years before the landing of the Pilgrims at Plymouth.

In 1623 the first permanent *agricultural* colony was established in New Netherlands, as this province was called by the Hollanders. But the first object of the colonists was trade.

For a period of twelve years the exiled English Puritans dwelt safely and in Christian fellowship with their Protestant brethren at Leyden, in Holland. These twelve years spent there in security were surely not spent in vain, for from that place of their retreat the Puritan came hither, and planted his colony at Plymouth Rock, while the Hollanders brought their institutions to New Netherlands.

We gratefully acknowledge the agency of both in laying

the foundation of our institutions. We strongly deny a monopoly of praise to either. All the good we possess did not come out of the cabin of the Mayflower; but Providence gathered choice materials from the various nations of Europe, and brought them to these western shores to lay the foundation of a mighty nation, and to fulfill his vast designs.

It was in the year 1640, more than two hundred years ago, that these hardy pioneers entered the Minisink Valley, put up their log-huts on the banks of the Delaware, and soon made the fertile soil and the buried minerals contribute to their wants and their wealth.

Chancellor Kent, in a discourse before the New York Historical Society, in 1828, thus describes the character of these first colonists and their descendants:

"The Dutch settlers of New Netherlands were grave, temperate, firm, persevering men, who brought with them the industry, the economy, the simplicity, the integrity, and the bravery of their Belgic sires; and with those virtues they imported the lights of the Roman civil law, and the purity of the Protestant faith."

All the events in the life of these early settlers, their movements and enterprises, their coming and going, their hopes and disappointments, for nearly ninety years, were left unrecorded. The very existence of their settlement in the Minisink was unknown to the Government at Philadelphia until the year 1729.

In the following year, the authorities in Pennsylvania, who regarded the Minisink Valley as a part of their charter, sent an agent, the famous surveyor, Nicholas Scull, to visit the valley and report to them what these Dutch settlers were doing there. Through this agent the first authentic accounts were received. He was accompanied by one John Lukens, then but a lad, who afterwards was made surveyor-general of the State. Lukens, many years after, described their journey northward from Philadelphia through Bucks and Northampton counties, guided by the Indians whom they hired for this purpose, there being no white settlers on the route. It seems to have been one of great peril and fatigue, and they had infinite difficulty in leading their horses through the water gap to the Minisink Flats. These Flats they found all settled by the Hollanders. They were hospitably entertained by the venerable Samuel Dupuis. Through the accounts received from him they became well satisfied that the first settlements in this valley were many years older than William Penn's charter.

They learned, also, that the Hollanders had purchased their lands of the Indians. These Indians were called Minguas, and were also known as the Minsies, having taken their name from the valley in which they lived—Minsies being a corruption, as it would seem, of Minisink, which means, as they inform us, "a drained lowland."

It was the Indian belief that this valley was once the bed of an extensive lake, but that it broke through the mountains that confined it at the spot now known as the Water Gap. Strange that these Hollanders should have lighted upon a spot with such a name, which would remind them so pleasantly of the dykes and drains of their native land.

The story of their earliest attempts to colonize and settle in these parts was thus narrated by Samuel Dupuis to the Philadelphia agents: "Not very long after the landing of the first colonists at New Amsterdam some of the more enterprising determined to penetrate the country in search of minerals. With this purpose they followed the course of the Hudson, northward as far as Esopus, now called Kingston, where they landed and explored westwardly, through the Mamakating Valley, for about fifty miles. Here they discovered a mine of lead ore. Encouraged by this success, they continued their explorations, and about fifty miles farther on they found traces of copper which soon proved to be abundant and valuable. This was on the Delaware River where the mountain nearly approaches the lower point of Pahaquarry Flat."

"The reports of their success soon attracted other settlers within the limits of our territory. They commenced at once the construction of a road from their new settlement on the Delaware to the town of Esopus on the Hudson, a distance of *one hundred miles*."

This road was so substantially built that it is still a public thoroughfare, and will remain for ages an enduring monument to the energy and perseverance of those hardy pioneers. It was the first road of any considerable length made in this country; it was built without Government aid, though its course ran through a howling wilderness, and its construction must have been attended with immense difficulties. It was the private enterprise of a few men, who pushed it to completion in the hope of the wealth which would come from their mineral discoveries. This hope of theirs was destined to a grievous disappointment by the conquest of New Netherlands, by the English, in the year 1664. Many then abandoned their mines, and returned to their native land; yet not all, for among those that remained, or that afterwards returned, may have been the ancestors of the most worthy names in our county—the Dupuis, Ryersons, Westbrooks, and Schoonermakers.

"Here, then," as Mr. Edsall remarks (from whose admirable Centennial Address we have already quoted so freely), "we have clearly established the time when the first settlement in Sussex County was made. Log cabins had been built here, orchards planted, mines worked, and the ore transported for one hundred miles over an excellent road, when the site of Philadelphia was a wilderness."

Not very long after the breaking up of the first colony of Hollanders, by the British conquest, another colony of the same people came over, and, passing along the mine-road which their predecessors had constructed, settled in the same district. These were driven, we are told, from their native homes by religious persecution; but the accounts of this second emigration are confused and obscure.

Names of Huguenot-French origin are also found upon the early records of the Minisink region; these emigrants were driven from France, in 1685, by the revocation of the Edict of Nantz. Among these are found the names of Gumaer, Cuddeback, Dekay, Dildine, and Bevier, well known among us at the present day.

Nearly a quarter of a century had now passed, during

which time much progress had been made in discovery and in material improvements by those early settlers.

England having been victorious in its war with Holland, all their North American possessions had been ceded to them by the Dutch. Charles the Second had immediately issued a grant of them to his brother, the Duke of York, who had given his own name to the largest and most important of the ceded provinces, and had immediately parted with that portion then first and still known as the State of New Jersey. The sale was made in 1664 to Lord Berkeley and Sir George Carteret for the sum of ten shillings. On the same day Philip Carteret, brother of Sir George, received a commission as first governor of New Jersey. A constitution was soon formed, and efforts made to induce colonists to come and settle in the new province. Notwithstanding all these efforts its growth for many years was slow, and the flow of emigration exceedingly small.

Ninety years from this date, when Sussex County was organized and chartered, the whole population of the State of New Jersey is said to have been less than forty-eight thousand, of whom not more than five or six hundred were living within the limits of this county. At that time there could not have been found either school or meeting-house. There were hardly any roads; wagons were unknown except in the Minisink region, and they were constructed with little or no iron; the wheels, made of thick felloes, were held together by wooden pins, without tires. Sleds were in general use, roughly put together and shod with wood. Flax, tow, and rawhide were the materials of which harness was made.

It is said that at that early date there was but one grist-mill, which was somewhere near the confluence of the Flatbrook and the Delaware. This mill, like all those which were built for twenty-five years after, performed no operation but that of grinding; the bolting was done by hand, for which purpose seives were an indispensable domestic utensil.

The plough and the harrow differed but little from those in use forty or fifty years ago. Flails were in general use, and horses were occasionally employed to tread out the grain.

Scythes, cradles, and fanning mills came into use simultaneously about the year 1750.

The social life of the people is thus graphically described by Rev. Mr. Kanouse:

"In the log cabins of the pioneers of this county there was no furniture to dazzle without profit. Oiled paper might serve for window glass, a pail of water for a mirror, a pine-knot for a candle, and the wheel and the loom made the music of the family. The father supplied the flax and the wool, and the fair hands of our mothers and their daughters furnished the cloth and the ready-made garment. They were rich in their own resources. Their wants were few and simple. The trencher and the wooden bowl were the china, and pewter was the silverware of the family, with milk and water for their tea, a burnt crust for their coffee, and brown bread for their cake. Of course, with such a generation, the physician had but little to do. If privation and toil were their companions, health was the reward."

In the year 1735, three brothers named Green came and settled in that part of Greenwich now known as Oxford township. They were soon followed by the McKees, McMurtrees, Stewarts, Hulls, Swayzes, and others, most of whom were Scotch-Irish Presbyterians. Here, as a consequence, the first Presbyterian Church of the county was erected in the year 1744. Rev. James Campbell was the first minister.

The celebrated David Brainerd, whose missionary labors among the Indians often called him to this vicinity, subsequently preached in this church. For some time he lived at a place now known as Lower Mount Bethel, about five miles from Belvidere. The site of the cabin occupied by himself and his interpreter is still shown to the traveler. All the territory now comprised in old Sussex was at first treated by our provincial authorities as belonging to what was then called West Jersey.

In 1709 an act was passed by the Assembly defining the boundaries of the several counties into which the Province was then divided.

This county of Sussex was at first comprehended within

the limits of Burlington. Four years later Hunterdon was erected into a county and separated from Burlington. For the next twenty-five years this section formed a part of Hunterdon, when Morris County was set off and chartered; still the name of Sussex County was unknown. For fifteen years these hills and valleys formed a part of Morris.

Previous to this there had been within the limits of this county several important Indian settlements: one in what was afterwards known as Greenwich township, near Phillipsburg; another on the present site of Belvidere; a third near Greensville, and a fourth near the village of Lafayette. But many of them had sold their lands to the white settlers, and had moved further north. Little danger, therefore, being apprehended, emigrants flowed in somewhat faster. In the year 1750, the settlers, regarding themselves as sufficiently numerous, petitioned the Provincial Assembly to divide the county and allow them the liberty of building a court-house and jail. This request was deemed reasonable on account of the inconvenient distance of Morristown, the county seat, where all the public business was transacted.

On the 8th day of June, in the year of our Lord 1753, the act incorporating the County of Sussex was passed by the Assembly.

This name was given to it by Jonathan Belcher, Esq., then Governor of the province, in compliment to the Duke of Newcastle, whose family seat was in the County of Sussex, England. Belcher was a native of New England, and had been Governor of Massachusetts. He was a descendant of an excellent family, a man of rich and varied culture, which he had received both in this country and in Europe. His name is worthy of honorable mention, and should be familiar to the people of Sussex County.

About this time the territory embraced within the limits of this and the neighboring counties was first divided into *townships*, and something like municipal organization was attempted among their scattered populations. These provisions, though imperfect, were greatly needed, and were very welcome to the people. The four townships first formed were Wallpack, New

Town, Hardwick, and Greenwich. The two former covered the whole of the present area of this county, excepting that portion now known as Stillwater and Green, which then formed part of Hardwick and Greenwich.

The act incorporating the county granted all the rights and privileges enjoyed by other counties, except the choice of Representatives to the Assembly, as the State Legislature was then called. It provided, however, that all persons legally qualified might, at the proper time, appear at Trenton, and there vote with the freeholders of Morris and Hunterdon for two members of the Assembly.

On account of the distance of Trenton our county was thus practically deprived of direct representation, and so continued for a period of fifteen years On the 10th of March, 1768, an act was passed authorizing the freeholders of this county to choose two representatives for themselves. The first election was held in the year 1772, when Thomas Van Horn and Nathaniel Pettit were chosen; Pettit served until the Declaration of Independence; Van Horn died the year before. The new State constitution, then formed, gave to Sussex three members of Assembly and one of the Legislative council.

In about the year 1750, one Henry Hairlocker, a Hollander, settled near the present site of Newton. His cabin was built where Major John R. Pettit's dwelling recently stood. There was, at that time, not a cabin visible for miles around. The village of Newton was unthought of, and might never have been founded but for the act of the Legislature, which established the county seat on the plantation occupied by this Hairlocker. This made a market for building lots, and a tavern was put up without delay.

On the 20th day of November, 1753, the first Court of Justice held in this county was opened in the house of Jonathan Pettit, in Hardwick township. The first judges of this court were Jonathan Robeson, Abraham Van Campan, John Anderson, Jonathan Pettit, and Thomas Woolverton, who received their commission from George the Second, King of England. The same men were likewise empowered at that time to act as Justices of the Peace. Nothing was done at the first session of this court—in the absence of grand and petit jurors—but to grant tavern licenses and fix the rates at which innkeepers should dispose of their liquors and provender. At this time, and for at least fifty years afterwards, the business of tavern keeping was a stepping-stone to public distinction. Nearly all the early judges, justices, sheriffs, etc., were innkeepers.

In 1754—the year following the organization of the county and of the first court—a jail was built near Jonathan Pettit's tavern, on the farm of Samuel Green. The total cost of this building was £41 3s. 1d. (about $200). Being so cheaply constructed, prisoners easily escaped, so that more than fourteen times the cost of the building was paid out by the county, in the first nine years, to the creditors of escaped debtors.

The sum of £100 was assessed upon the county each year, three-fourths of which was expended in bounties for the destruction of wolves. In 1754 and 1755 about £120 was paid for the scalps of these ferocious beasts, or nearly three times as much as it cost to erect the jail.

Shortly after the county was erected, three *precincts*, as they were then called, were added to the four original townships. From Newton was formed Wantage; from Greenwich, Oxford and Mansfield-Woodhouse, Hardwick and Wallpack retaining their original limits. Within a few years the increase of population made further divisions necessary. In 1759, four years after the first precincts were formed, Montague was set off from Wallpack by royal patent; three years later, Sandyston and Hardyston were formed, the latter from the northern portion of Newton. Two years after, Knowlton was set off from Oxford; and in 1782 Independence from Hardwick; Vernon from Hardyston ten years later; Frankford from Newton in 1797, and, in the following year, Byram from Newton. These divisions multiplied the four original townships to fifteen, the number at the close of the last century, and there were no other townships formed until the county of Warren was set off from Sussex in the year 1824.

The area of the county at that time was nearly one thousand square miles, with a population of about thirty-five thousand. This large and rapid increase suggested the necessity of erecting another county for the accommodation of the towns on its southern border. That portion of Sussex thus set off was called Warren, and included six of the fifteen townships, viz.: Greenwich. Oxford, Mansfield-Woodhouse, Hardwick, Knowlton, and Independence. Six years after the separation, Warren County contained, by the census of 1830, over eighteen thousand and Sussex over twenty thousand. Since 1824 six townships have been added to the nine left to Sussex: they are Andover, Green, Hampton, Lafayette, Sparta, and Stillwater.

To show the progress made in this county, it has been said that in 1765, when the court-house was opened for public business in Newton, there were but eight small houses of worship, which altogether had cost less than $3,000. Twenty years ago there were in the same territory ninety-two, the value of which was nearly $200,000. At the same early period there were not more schools in the county than churches. This number had increased, within the period mentioned, to two hundred and thirty-seven, besides several classical academies for young men and seminaries for young ladies.

On the 8th day of January, 1796, the first newspaper was issued in Sussex, entitled the "Farmers' Journal and Newton Advertiser," but it died in about a year from its birth for want of sustenance. From this it is evident that our fathers were not a reading people. Now there are in our county three flourishing papers issued weekly—the "New Jersey Herald," and the "Sussex Register," both in Newton, and the "Deckertown Independent." There is no surer test than this of the general enterprise and thrift of a community.

Sussex County, during the Revolutionary era, shared a full proportion of the sturdy freeborn spirit which conceived and the iron will and persistent energy which carried to completion the liberation of our country from British despotism.

In consequence of the violent conduct of a few outlaws who took advantage of the retreats afforded by our mountains, Sussex has been stigmatized as a "Nest of Tories," but no county in the State can show so fair a proportion of loyal citizens who faithfully adhered to the principles of the oath administered to them by the State. But in the annals of the county enough is found to vindicate the patriotism of our citizens and to show the general unanimity with which they embraced the cause of freedom.

The area of this county is five hundred and sixty-seven square miles; it is twenty-seven miles long and twenty-one broad. It is bounded north by Orange County, N. Y.; east, by Passaic and Morris; south, by Warren; and west, by the Delaware River.

The population by townships, at the last census, is as follows:

Township	Population	Township	Population
Andover,	1,126	Montague,	932
Byram,	1,332	Newton,	2,403
Frankford,	1,776	Sandyston,	1,230
Green,	868	Sparta,	2,031
Hardyston,	1,669	Stillwater,	1,632
Hampton,	1,023	Vernon,	1,979
Lafayette,	884	Wallpack,	647
Wantage,	3,636.		
Total,	23,168.		

ANDOVER TOWNSHIP.

In March, 1864, the townships of Andover and Hampton were set off from that of Newton, by which its dimensions were reduced to a very small circle covered by the town and its immediate suburbs.

Andover has an area of twenty square miles; it is five miles north and south, and four east and west. It has Newton and Hampton on the north, Byram and Green on the south; the former with Sparta extending also along its eastern side, and the latter on its western.

The Sussex Railroad, from its junction with the Morris and Essex at Waterloo, runs northerly through this township towards Newton and beyond. Since it was built the thrift and business of Andover have greatly increased.

Its population, in 1870, was 1,126.

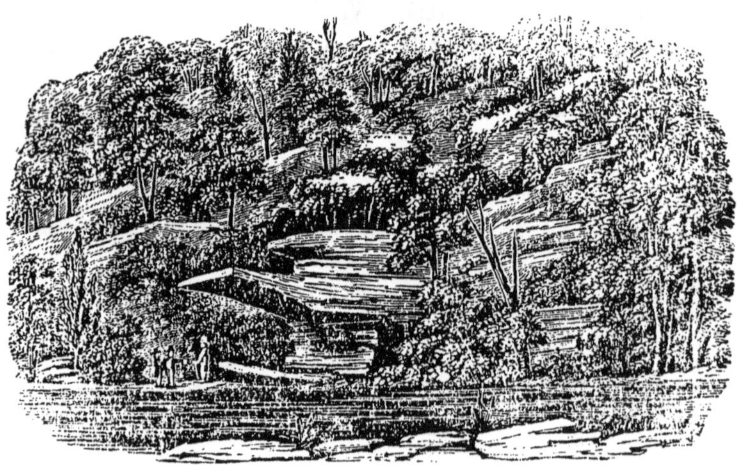

MOODY'S ROCK.

This picture represents a spot familiar to all in that vicinity and noted throughout the county. It is situated in the northwestern part of the township, by the Big Muckshaw Pond. It was here that Bonnel Moody and his company of Tories found shelter during the Revolutionary struggle. This wild and secluded spot, to which they resorted in times of danger, was so situated that with a stock of provisions he and the few royalists associated with him were perfectly safe from attack. Screened by the projecting rock, or hidden by the thick foliage of overhanging branches of trees, they could watch unobserved the coming of an enemy, whilst a deep swamp, twenty rods wide, almost impassable, protected the approach to the spot on three sides.

A story is told of this bold and lawless Royalist, that once he entered the town of Newton, at midnight, and demanded of the jailer the keys of the prison. When the scared keeper had handed them over, Moody released all the prisoners. Some years since a key was found near that spot, which is said to be the very one which he got from the jailer. Moody is said to have come from Kingwood, in the County of Hunterdon, in this State; he was employed by the British to get recruits in this region, among the Royalists, and to act as spy on the movements of the Whigs. He attempted to create divisions among them, and weaken their confidence in the leaders of the Revolution. Many wonderful stories are told about him which cannot be narrated here.

Besides Andover, there are in this township four other smaller places—Springdale, Whitehall, Brighton, and Pinkneyville.

ANDOVER.

Andover is in the lower extremity of the county, six miles south of Newton, on the Sussex Railroad.

In 1714, William Penn, having, by a warrant from the Council of Proprietors, acquired title to a large tract of land in this county, became owner of what was afterwards known as the Andover Iron Mine.

Soon after this the mine, with the lands adjoining, passed into the hands of an English Company, from the County of Sussex, in England. This company worked the mine until the second year of the Revolutionary War. At this time Congress having been informed that iron and steel of the best quality were manufactured here, and used for purposes of war by the enemy, directed the Government of New Jersey to secure the mine and work it for the benefit of the United States. For five years subsequently it furnished iron and steel for the Continental Army. This mine is situated about one and a half miles from the present village. For many years after the close of the war it lay deserted, but is now again in good working order under the direction of the Andover Iron Company. This was the first mine opened in the county, and attracted attention to the mineral resources which have since been developed so richly in our hills and valleys.

In 1814 Andover contained only a mill, a blacksmith's shop, and three or four houses. The mill was built by Joseph Northrup, who owned all the tract of land known as "Furnace Tract," which then included the site of the village.

Little improvement was made in the village until about thirty years ago, and indeed it may be said to have been built within the last fifteen years. The buildings all have a fresh appearance, and indicate the thrift and enterprise of the people. It is the business place of the township. For country residences for city people it affords excellent advantages. The scenery in the neighborhood is very fine, the air clear and healthful, and the railroad facilities excellent, as it connects daily with five trains to New York, and the depot is located centrally. The present population is estimated at three hundred

It contains a Methodist and a Presbyterian Church, several good stores, an hotel, two blacksmith shops, and a tin store. A steam saw-mill, belonging to Mr. Benjamin Totten is situated about a mile above Andover, on the railroad, and there is another, driven by water-power, belonging to the Hon. Wm. M. Iliff.

METHODIST CHURCH OF ANDOVER.

The first church erected in the place was built by the Bapists in 1834, assisted by a provision in the will of a Miss Hill. But the congregation being small and unable to sustain the worship, it was (after an effort of nearly twenty years to hold it) sold to Wm. M. Iliff, who conveyed it to the Methodist

Protestants in 1855. They held it for a time, when it came into the possession of the Methodist Episcopal denomination, and was at first supplied by pastors from the Newton charge. It was afterwards remodeled and improved; it is now under the pastoral charge of Rev. W. E. Blakesley.

PRESBYTERIAN CHURCH OF ANDOVER.

On the seventh of April, 1858, an application was made to Presbytery, by the Rev. M. Barrett, for the organization of a Presbyterian Church in Andover. A committee was then appointed, which met on the 25th of September following, at the Academy, in Andover, when the church was organized with welve members.

In the following month Rev. J. Sanford Smith accepted a call from this church and became the first pastor, continuing in this relation until the Summer of 1862, during which time the church was built. The church had then seventy-five members. After Mr. Smith left, the pulpit was filled by stated supplies until October, 1871, when Rev. Edward Webb acaccepted a call, and was installed on the 24th of November following. In 1869, through the influence of Rev. David Conway, a basement was built, the church fenced and shade trees planted. In the following year a bell was purchased and placed in the tower. The church stands on a hill north-east of the village.

SPRINGDALE

Is is a little village lying half way between Newton and Andover on the Pequest River.

The situation of the place is pleasant and desirable. The water-power, which is said to be good, is utilized by a gristmill.

There are, besides, eight or ten dwellings, and a shoolhouse, in which religious services are held on Sabbath by ministers of several denominations alternately.

BRIGHTON.

The name given to a small number of houses about one mile below Andover, near the borders of Green.

WHITEHALL

Is a little hamlet about a mile south of Andover, on the Sussex Railroad. The largest building was formerly a tavern where the Newark and Oswego stages used to stop.

PINKNEYVILLE.

This is a little mining village, with only a few small cottages. It is in the upper or north-eastern part of the township.

BYRAM TOWNSHIP.

This township lies on the southern boundary of the county. Sparta is north, the Musconnetcong River south, and Lake Hopatcong on the east, separating it from Morris County; it is bounded west by Andover and Green. It has an average length of eight, and a width of five miles. Lake Hopatcong is a most beautiful sheet of water nearly six miles in length, and in one place more than two miles wide. The Musconnetcong River, flowing from it, is used as a feeder for the Morris Canal. The Sussex Railroad, connecting at Waterloo with the Morris and Essex Railroad, passes through the south-west corner of Byram. A branch of the Musconnetcong rises in the northern part of the township, and flows down through the centre, which, with numerous small ponds, the lake and river on its southern and eastern boundary, gives to the township an inexhaustible supply of water.

The surface is mountainous, and contains a large quantity of iron ore.

ROSEVILLE,

In the centre of the township, consisting of some ten or twelve houses, was built for the accommodation of miners who worked in that vicinity some years since.

The other villages in Byram are Stanhope and Waterloo.

STANHOPE.

Stanhope is situated on the Musconnetcong River, at the extreme southern point of the township. Its history dates back to the commencement of the present century. At that time there were here two iron forges, a grist-mill, two saw-mills, a blacksmith shop, and about a dozen dwelling houses; there were then no hotel, church, school-house, or store in the place, but in 1810 or '12 the Methodists organized a society and held meetings at private dwellings.

In 1815 the first hotel was opened by Richard Lewis, at the corner where John M. Knight, Esq., now keeps his well-known house. A few years later a school-house was built, which, in the absence of any church, was used as a place of worship.

The first store was a small one, kept by Mahlon F. Dickerson, after which the large stone store. built by John Bell, was erected.

The chief attraction of the place, at this early date, was the orges, the ore for which was brought from a distance of six or eight miles.

The Morris Canal, begun in July, 1825, and completed from the Delaware to Newark in August, 1831, made Stanhope a depot for the shipment of wood and charcoal. The Morris and Essex Railroad extension, completed about eighteen years ago, from Dover to Hackettstown, greatly increased the business importance of the village.

In 1844, ten years previous to this extension, the amount of capital invested in the manufacture of iron was about $30,000. This sum has since greatly increased, and the principal feature and centre of attraction, now, is the Musconnetcong Iron Works, which are described in another part of this work. Dr. G. G. Palmer is the superintendent of these works.

THE CANAL.

A charter for the construction of a canal, to be called the Morris Canal, was obtained in December, 1824. It was commenced in July of the following year; was seven years in construction, and was completed from the Delaware River to Newark, in August, 1831.

Greenwood Lake and Pompton Feeders were finished in 1837.

The dimensions of the canal were then—bottom, width at twenty feet; at top water-line, thirty feet; depth of water, four feet.

The first boats carried only an average of eighteen tons gross weight.

A new company was organized in 1844, which commenced enlarging the canal. Since 1860, the boats carry an average of seventy tons. The total cost of building and enlarging, to 1860, had amounted to $5,100,000. In 1866 it was extended to Jersey City.

The principal business of the canal is the freighting of coal from Lehigh, Scranton, and other mines to the east; returning westward, ore from Morris and Sussex counties is brought to Stanhope, Easton, Phillipsburg, and to the furnaces along the Lehigh.

Stanhope now, with its iron works, canal, and railroad, has a bright prospect of progress and prosperity. Its population is increasing, and men of means and enterprise are its supporters. A new hotel has recently been built near the depot, and new dwellings are going up.

The district school is well sustained, and has an average attendance of one hundred scholars.

THE FIRST PRESBYTERIAN CHURCH OF STANHOPE.

This church was organized January 11th, 1838, by a committee from the Presbytery of Newark.

At that time there were twenty-eight members, mostly from the church at Succasunna Plains.

The minister of the latter place, Rev. Joseph Moore, had preached in the village school-house once every month, and at his suggestion, the church was organized. Mr. Moore became their first pastor. The church was not built until 1844. It cost about $2,000. In the following year, when the church was dedicated, no debt remained on the building. It was enlarged and its interior very much improved during the pastorate of the Rev. James Morton,

In 1870, Rev. John Jay Craine took the charge, and acted as Stated Supply until August, 1871. He was installed on the 29th of that month, and is the present pastor of the church. It is small in numbers, and has been often aided by the Board of Home Missions. Its prospects, however, are improving, and the members hope soon to become self-sustaining.

STANHOPE M. E. CHURCH.

The records of this church have been lost. Rev. Theo. S. Haggerty, the present pastor, says: "The society was organized, and the first trustees elected on the 21st of August, 1843. Andrew Rose, John Rowland, and five others were made trustees, and Amos Smith, A. A. Smalley, and A. J. King, a building committee. Among the first pastors were Rev. Messrs. Decker and Lawhead."

WATERLOO.

This place was originally called Old Andover. It is situated in the southern portion of Byram.

Waterloo is probably one of the oldest villages in the township; it was within the tract of land located by William Penn, in this part of the county, and, with the Andover Blast Furnace and Mine, was the district which was disposed of by him to the English Company before referred to.

At that time there was in this place a four-fire forge, and the iron manufactured was carried down the valley of the Musconnetcong to Durham on the Delaware.

The forge was situated a few yards north-east of the grist-mill of Messrs. S. T. Smith and Brothers, and the walls of the old coal-house form a part of this building. While the forge was in blast there was a grist and saw-mill in running order. The walls of the latter may still be seen a short distance east of the old forge site.

In 1848–9 a mule road was constructed from Andover Mine to Waterloo, over which the ore was carried and deposited in canal boats which conveyed it to Phillipsburg. This was the first railroad built in the country, but was abandoned, when, through the untiring efforts of Hon. A. S. Hewitt, the Sussex Railroad was constructed.

After the Morris Canal was in operation, and before the Sussex Railroad was built, Waterloo was quite an extensive freighting depot. Merchandise was brought from New York by the canal, and was carted from this place throughout the counties of Sussex and Warren.

There are large quantities of iron ore deposited in the vicinity of Waterloo, and, at the present time, the Lehigh Iron Company is working a vein of rich ore measuring from eight to ten feet, on the lands of Peter Smith.

To the west of Waterloo, on lands formerly owned by Job Brookfield, is the Waterloo Mine, operated by the Musconnetcong Iron Company at Stanhope. This ore is also very pure, and the mine looks promising.

The surface around Waterloo is mountainous, on account of which the air is remarkably pure and healthful, and the scenery is unsurpassed. The railroad communications are good, making the situation a desirable one.

The place contains a store, hotel, and a blacksmith shop. A fine large dwelling house has been recently built here by Mr. Peter Smith.

In the year 1859, during the pastorate of Rev. G. T. Jackson, a neat little church was erected by the Methodists. It stands at the base of the mountain. Services are now conducted on the Sabbath by the Rev. Wm. H. McCormick of Alamuchi.

FRANKFORD TOWNSHIP.

Frankford township has an average length of nine miles and a width of five.

It is bounded north by Wantage, south by Hampton, east by Lafayette, and west by Sandyston. The Blue Mountains, on the western boundary, form the separating line from Sandyston. Collver's Gap, a beautiful pass through these mountains, is situated between Long and Collver's Ponds, on the stage road from Branchville to Port Jervis.

Frankford, like most of the townships in the county, produces great quantities of butter, the quality of which is not surpassed by any that is sent to New York city markets.

The north-west is stony and uneven, but the soil throughout the township is extremely fertile, and well adapted to the raising of cereals and vegetables.

Augusta, Branchville, Papakating or Pellettown, and Wykertown, are the post villages of the township.

AUGUSTA.

Augusta is situated on the east branch of the Paulinskill, one mile and a half below Branchville. More than half a century ago Augusta was the principal trading post for a district extending many miles around.

Before Branchville could count six houses, Augusta was a place of some importance, with a store kept by Col. John Gustin, a Presbyterian Church, and the stables of the great Newark and Owego Stage Company, where considerable business of the road was transacted.

Augusta, to-day, is very much as Branchville was fifty years ago. There is a blacksmith and carpenter's shop in the place, and a school-house has been recently built on the grounds belonging to the church. Quite an affair happened in the earlier history of this town, which is worth mention here:

Thomas P. Gustin, son of the colonel, becoming financially embarrassed while in business with his brother, in New York, returned to Augusta. He was followed there by his creditors, who requested Coroner Ephraim Green to apprehend him, Gustin, who was seated in the store, knowing the object of Green, sprang over the counter, and, seizing a pistol, fired at him, the ball entering his leg near the knee. For some time his life was despaired of, but after a painful illness he recovered. Gustin immediately escaped to the West. Green, after his recovery, was elected sheriff of the county, and subsequently county clerk. He was for many years President of the Sussex Bank in Newton.

THE PRESBYTERIAN CHURCH OF AUGUSTA.

The ground on which the church stands was deeded to a body of trustees, by Col. John Gustin, for such time as it should be used and occupied by them.

In 1827, a contract for the church was given to Abram Bray, and the building was erected by his brother Richard. Rev. Enos Osbourn was sent by the Home Missionary Society to labor in the place, and to ascertain the strength of the organization. He was succeeded by Rev. Burr Baldwin, who remained but a short time, when Presbytery sent Rev. Mr. Conkling, who superintended the raising of subscriptions for the new building, and became the first pastor. At this time there was no Presbyterian Church either at Branchville or Lafayette. Services were, however, held at both places in private houses on alternate Sabbaths.

In 1856 the Presbyterian Church of Branchville was built, and the congregation worshiped in it, making the Augusta Church merely an outpost.

BRANCHVILLE.

Branchville is a town of six hundred inhabitants, situated two miles above Augusta, on the west branch of the Paulenskill, which takes its rise at Collver's Pond, one and a half miles above the village, reaching it at a fall of three hundred feet. Collver's Pond is supported by Long Pond, so that few towns have a water-power affording superior advantages to manufacturers.

Branchville was settled about the year 1700, by emigrants, principally from Connecticut. Ten years before that date, however, one lonely dwelling might have been seen, that of William Beemer. The village has been mostly built within the last fifty years. Among the early settlers were Colt, Dewitt, Beemer, Price, and Gustin.

The land on which the town, is built, then belonged to James Haggerty, who left it to his son Uzal C. Haggerty, by whom it was sold to Judge John Bell, Joseph Stoll, and Samuel Price. About 1820 they divided it into building lots. It was named Branchville by the school teacher of that district—Samuel Bishop. Previous to this it had been known by several names. Brantown appears to have been the most popular.

Farmer Johnson kept the first hotel; Dr. John Beach, the first store, in the house now occupied by the mother of Wm. H. Bell, Esq.

The recent extension of the Sussex Railroad to Branchville has given quite an impetus to business, and for a time the town grew rapidly; but too much was expected, and at present it suffers from the incapacity of certain men in whom the people placed their entire confidence, and many half finished schemes remain as evidences of their miscalculations; but owing to the superior attractions to manufacturers, the town will doubtless eventually rise from its present depressed condition.

Messrs. F. Barbier & Co. recently put up some new machinery, for making, by a new process, calf skin, said to be equal to the best French. If successful, it may give an impetus to the growth and commercial importance of the town.

Branchville contains three grist-mills. The one owned by Mr. V. H. Crisman has four run of stone, and thirty-three feet fall of water, grinding last year fifty thousand bushels of grain.

A woolen factory, four stories high, was erected some years since, but at present is not in operation. The tannery of Messrs. F. Barbier & Co. occupies the basement.

There are several stores, two harnessmakers, blacksmiths' and wheelwrights' shops, a tin, and a cooper's shop. A sash and blind manufactory was built with all the necessary appliances, but has not yet gone into operation. The prospects of Branchville are brighter now than for a long time past.

There is in the place a live temperance organization, which is doing much good.

There are two public halls—Dunning's and Bedell's—which furnish ample accommodation for literary, political, and religious gatherings.

THE PRESBYTERIAN CHURCH OF BRANCHVILLE.

This organization originated from the Augusta Church. The building was erected in 1856, and was dedicated in the spring of the following year. The sermon was preached on this occasion by Rev. Jas. F. Tuttle. For a short time Rev. A. A. Haines, supplied the pulpit, after which Rev. Geo. W. Lloyd became pastor, and remained eight years. The congregation is large, and, under the present pastorate of Rev. Wm. H. Belden, is in a prosperous condition.

M. E. CHURCH.

A few years since the Methodists in and around Branchville made an effort to erect a house of worship, and sufficient money having been raised preparations were made for building. The frame was put up and partly enclosed, when, in a heavy gale of wind, it blew down. This accident left the church in debt, and no effort has since been made to rebuild. The lot on which the old foundation stands belongs to the Church. The Methodist brethren worshiped for some time in the

UNION CHURCH

which stands on the summit of the hill, back of the village, but since 1870 they have used both Dunning's and Bedell's Halls.

FRANKFORD PLAIN CHURCH.

This building was put up about sixty-five years ago. situated about half way between Branchville and Wykertown. It is a Methodist organization, and has always been a very flourishing church. It once belonged to the Lafayette charge.

PAPAKATING, OR PELLETTOWN.

The district and town known as Papakating is situated in the most beautiful valley in Frankford. It is three miles in length and about two in width. The soil in this valley is exceedingly fertile.

WYKERTOWN

Is a small post village three and a half miles north-east from Branchville. It is situated on a branch of the Papakating River, and contains a blacksmith and cooper's shop, and about a dozen dwelling houses.

GREEN TOWNSHIP.

Green township has Hampton and Andover on the north-east; Byram is south-east; its south-west boundary line separates it from Warren County; its north-west from Stillwater. The surface is uneven, but not so ragged and mountainous as many of the surrounding townships. The Pequest River and numerous small streams water it throughout, making it exceedingly fertile and well suited for agricultural purposes. A low range of hills partly separate it from Stillwater. The villages within its limits are Greensville, Huntsville, Tranquility, and Hunt's Mills.

GREENSVILLE.

This village was first settled in 1770 by the Greens and Shiners. The town was named after Ephraim Green who erected several buildings, one of which was a tan-yard, which was opposite the present hotel, where a barn now stands. This business was carried on suuccssfully until 1832. Mr. Amos Shiner, one of the first settlers, erected a still-house and carried on his business, for many years, on the present site of the wheelwright shop.

About two years since the name of the post-office was changed to Lincoln. Originally there was an Indian settlement near the site of the village of which nothing definite is known. The little stone building, just below the village, on the road to Canadatown, now occupied as a dwelling-house was used until recently for the village school, and had been for many generations. When the church was built a room was prepared over it for school purposes. The ruins of Shiner's old blacksmith shop still remain. The place now contains an hotel, a wheelwright shop, a store and shoe shop.

GREENSVILLE UNION CHAPEL.

This building was commenced in 1866, and was dedicated on the 14th of November, of the following year. Services had been previously held in the school-house, but the accommodations both for school and religious purposes being insufficient, a united effort was made by the school board, and by the Methodists and Presbyterians, to build a Union Chapel, which should accommodate all. This effort resulted in the erection of the building, without delay, at a cost of about $3,500. In 1869 a bell was procured, at a cost of about $100.

HUNTSVILLE.

Huntsville is the name given to a small hamlet, containing not more than forty or fifty people, on the Pequest, two miles west of Andover. It has a store, a blacksmith's and a wheelwright's shop, a saw-mill, and a grist-mill. Recently a large substantial brick building has been erected here for a school.

Tranquility Meeting-House is a large well-built edifice belonging to the Methodists. It is about two miles south of Huntsville, and half a mile from Canadatown. It was finished in the year 1868, at a cost of about $10,000. It is now under the pastoral care of Rev. William H. McCormick, residing at Alamuchi.

CANADATOWN, OR TRANQUILITY.

This village was named from Amos H. Canada, who settled in the locality when it contained but two or three farm houses. It is called, by many, Tranquility, from the large Methodist Church near by. Mr. Canada built the grist-mill, the store, and several of the dwelling houses still standing. It is on the Pequest, about three miles south-west of Huntsville. A blacksmith's shop here does the work for Greensville as well as for this place.

HUNT'S MILLS.

This is a post village, sometimes called Washington, situated in the north-western corner of the township. Just here the surface is very hilly, and farming operations are carried on with unusual difficulty. The water-power, which is excellent, is used to drive two good sized mills, one for grist and the other for lumber.

HAMPTON TOWNSHIP.

Hampton was set off from Newton township in March, 1864. It was named from Jonathan Hampton—he who gave the land for the court-house at Newton, and by whose efforts and influence that place was preferred, before Stillwater, for the county seat.

It has Frankford on the north, Newton and Andover on the south, Lafayette on the east, Stillwater and Green on the west. Toward the north-west, as you approach the Blue Mountains, the surface becomes very rugged and hilly. The only villages are Balesville and Washingtonville, about a mile apart in the northern portion. The sole occupation of the people is farming and grazing, though the Paulinskill, which passes through it, affords excellent power.

The township contains 12,943 acres, and, according to the Assessor's Report for 1871, the total valuation of Taxable property was $90,990.

WASHINGTONVILLE.

This village was originally called Halsey's Corner, but for the past twenty years has been known by its present name. It is situatedthree miles north of Newton. Case's Hotel, the only hotel in the township, was built in 1848, by Sylvester P. Case, who kept it seven years when Mr. Benjamin S. Case became owner of the property, and, for the last twenty-three years, has been its proprietor. There is also in this place a a small grocery, wheelwright's and a blacksmith's shop. There are, besides, twelve or thirteen houses, with a population of about sixty. There is a school-house with an average attendance of fifty scholars.

BALESVILLE

Is a post village situated about a mile north-west of Washingtonville, on the Paulinskill. It was first settled in about the year 1800, by Henry and Peter Bale, and one or two others. At this time, however, the small mill, recently burnt down, was in operation. Immediately after their arrival they erected a larger grist-mill, a saw-mill, and a blacksmith's shop, which was worked by Peter Bale.

In about the year 1820, a woolen manufactory was built, and for two or three years turned out large quantities of woolen cloth. Since that time it has been used simply for a carding mill. This is the only mill of the kind now in operation in the county; and in years gone by, when farmers made most of their own garments, it was run night and day.

Pleasant Valley adjoins Balesville, and is the name of the post-office. The population of the two combined is about fifty.

The old blacksmith's shop is now no longer used. The old grist-mill, burnt down two or three years ago, has been rebuilt, and is now used as a saw-mill and turning establishment. The water-power is good. About twenty-four or twenty-five years ago a *Christian Church* was erected here. The first pastor was Rev. Alva Hermans. It has always had a good attendance, and has for its present pastor the Rev. George Searles.

HARDYSTON TOWNSHIP.

This township is eight miles long and five wide, bounded north by Vernon and Wantage; south, by Sparta; east, by Passaic and Morris counties; and west, by Wantage and Lafayette. Its population is about 1,700, consisting principally of miners.

The greater portion of the township is mountainous; the hills here are rich in mineral ore, both of iron and zinc.

The three principal villages, Franklin, Hamburgh and Hardystonville, are watered by the Wallkill, which runs through the township.

The Midland Railroad, recently completed from New York, passes through these three places, as also through Snufftown, a village on the east of the township. In the south-west corner, on a branch of the Wallkill, is a station of the Sussex Railroad called Monroe Corners.

FRANKLIN.

This place is ten miles north-east from Newton, and through the Midland and Sussex Railroads it is brought into direct communication with all points—north, south, east and west. It is situated on the Wallkill river. The mountains which surround it, contain an inexhaustible supply of iron and zinc.

The appearance of the place itself is very uninviting. The dwellings, almost all of them occupied by the miners, are small, and are scattered here and there, without any approach to order or plan of arrangement.

The largest blast furnace in the United States is now building here, and it is to be followed by two others of the same size. The ore to be smelted is brought from the mines by rail and there dumped into position; this furnace will produce 50,000 tons of pig iron annually. With those resources and facilities, and an unlimited capital to develop the exhaustless mineral wealth of the place, Franklin will doubtless increase in population and importance, and will be an influential centre in our county.

A new and excellent schoolhouse has been recently built, and is already well filled with a large number of children living in and around the place.

HAMBURG.

This village is situated in the northwestern portion of the township. It was originally called Lower Hamburg.

Hamburg, like many of the villages along the route of the Midland Railroad, has, since the completion of this road, grown both in population and importance. A number of new buildings have been recently erected. A chapel has been built by the Presbyterians, and services are now held in it by the Rev. A. A. Haines. This is a branch of the North Church. A neat little Methodist church has just been finished, and was dedicated in September, 1872. The size of this building is 22 x 42 feet, and cost $2,000.

The foundations of an Episcopal church have been laid, but nothing more will probably be done during the present year.

The Baptist church here, of which Rev. David Silver is pastor, is the oldest in the place; until the erection of their own churches the Methodists and Presbyterians held services in this building.

A fine large hotel has recently been put up; besides which there is the old "Hamburg House." Besides the buildings already mentioned it contains two grist mills, a lumber yard, blacksmith's shop and two or three stores. It has a population of about 250.

HARDYSTONVILLE

Was formerly called Upper Hamburg, but is now known only by its present name. It is two miles north of Franklin Furnace, and about a mile south of Hamburg. A fine water power is obtained here from a tributary of the Wallkill, upon which a grist mill has been put up. It has an hotel and about half a dozen houses.

SNUFFTOWN

Is a small village in the eastern portion of this township. The Midland Railroad passes through it. There are two hotels, two stores and a Methodist church here. This was built in 1826, and rebuilt in 1863. Rev. Jos. H. Timbrel of Sparta is the present pastor. The post-office and district, a mile or two east of the village, is called Stockholm.

LAFAYETTE TOWNSHIP.

Lafayette Township, named from the Marquis de Lafayette, was the first place in the Union which took the name of that nobleman. The township is situated near the centre of the county, and is watered throughout by the east branch of the Paulenskill. It is bounded north by Wantage, south by Hampton and Andover, east by Sparta and Hardyston, and west by Frankford and Hampton. Its average width is three miles and its length six. Lafayette and Lower Lafayette, which includes Statesville, are the villages of this township.

The village of Lafayette is beautifully situated on the east branch of the Paulenskill, about five miles northeast from Newton. It was organized about forty years ago.

In the year 1836 an iron foundry was built, and for many years was very successfully worked, the pig iron being drawn mostly from Franklin, but about ten years ago this business began to fall off, and so continued to until 1865 or '6, when it was entirely abandoned.

Fifty years ago nothing distinguished the locality but a store, a few houses, a grist and sawmill, both carried on under the same roof. This building was of logs, put together in the rough and ready style. The mill was built by Peter Bale. It was sufficient to meet all the wants of the people for many years; but, in 1826, increased business made the erection of a larger building and the purchasing of new machinery necessary, and the log mill, which was situated where two houses now stand, opposite the present mill and next to the foundry, was soon after torn down. This new frame structure was burned to the ground in 1858, and the present mill was built upon the same site.

Many years ago a still-house was built here, but at the extension of the Sussex Railroad to Branchville, the line of construction passing through the centre of the building, the apparatus was removed to the rear of the mill into an addition that was built for it. A part of the old building still remains on an embankment just above the track.

At the present time a good business is done at Mr. David Monroe's sash and blind manufactory, where about a dozen hands are employed. It has been in successful operation there for seventeen years. The annual business of this factory is about $15,000.

In 1871 a brick schoolhouse was erected here. There are two hotels, two blacksmith's and wheelwright's shops, besides grist-mill and still-house referred to.

A Good Templars' Lodge, consisting of ninety members has been formed, and meets regularly once a week.

LAFAYETTE BAPTIST CHURCH.

This was the first church edifice built in the place. It was erected in the year 1831. Rev. John Tisdeal, who had been preaching in the neighborhood, superintended the raising of subscriptions, and became the first pastor. The total cost was $11,000. For a few years the church continued in a very prosperous condition, and many members were received. Mr. Tisdeal, however, soon after removed to the Newton Baptist church, where events transpired which seriously retarded the prosperity of this church. From that time there was a gradual falling off in attendance and interest, which at last brought the church to a stand still.

For several years services were entirely suspended. Recently they have been recommenced, and are held regularly every Sabbath. Rev. Mr. Robinson is the present pastor.

LAFAYETTE M. E. CHURCH.

In 1841 the Methodist society commenced building a church for themselves. The edifice was put up at a cost of $1,550. In 1859 an addition was built, and a bell procured, which cost the society $1,000 more.

PRESBYTERIAN CHURCH OF LAFAYETTE.

This edifice was built in the years 1856–7. It was dedicated in July, 1867, with 14 members, and was organized there in the following month. These members were formerly connected with the North Church of Hardyston, and with the church of Augusta. Rev. Joel Campbell, who had been pastor of the North Church for eighteen years, was elected to preach as a stated supply.

In 1842 an effort had been made to put up a Presbyterian Church, and a committee was sent by the Presbytery to inquire into the expediency of building. After looking carefully into the strength of the organization it was decided not to attempt it at that time.

Mr. Campbell remained here as stated supply until early in 1872, when Rev. Jethro B. Woodward was called, and on May second was installed as the first pastor of the church. Mr. Campbell died the same month, twelve days after Mr. Woodward's installation, after an illness of only one week. Mr. Campbell had been forty-four years in the ministry, a faithful preacher of the Gospel and dearly beloved by all who knew him. His last public address was the charge given to the people at the installation of Mr. Woodward. Mr. Campbell, at his death, was seventy-five years of age. He was buried in the North Church Cemetery.

LOWER LAFAYETTE.

Lower Lafayette is situated about half a mile below Lafayette. In 1839 an iron foundry was built here, partly out of an old grist-mill, and called the Columbian Foundry. This property was bought by Mr. G. Collver, in 1842, where he has continued ever since. At the time Mr. Collver came here, in December, 1842, the place was hardly known by any name. In the following year he erected a grist and saw-mill. The former has recently had an addition.

The store situated in this place is also kept by Mr. Collver. The mill property of Messrs. Collver & Huston is situated in what is known in the locality as

STATESVILLE.

It was so called from a man of that name who lived there, but the designation is not generally recognized.

There is here a blacksmith's and wheelwright's shop. The former is a very old stand, having been in constant operation for forty years.

MONTAGUE TOWNSHIP.

Montague Township is situated in the extreme northwest corner of the county, bounded north by New York State, south by Sandyston, east by Wantage, and west by the Delaware, which separates it from Pennsylvania.

It is eight and one-half miles long, and has an average width of six miles.

The eastern portion of the township is very thinly settled, being covered by the Blue Mountain range, which separates it from Wantage, It is very valuable as timber land.

The village of Montague is the only post-office in the township.

The Hon. Isaac Bunnell, a well-known citizen of this township, related to the writer the following interesting account of an incursion which the Indians made into this township during the Revolution: Early one morning a party of twenty-one Indians crossed the Delaware in canoes and attacked a dwelling occupied by a family named Jobs. (This house has been recently torn down by Mr. Joseph Shimer, who is now erecting a dwelling on the same site.) There they killed three young men and took two women prisoners. They then crossed Shimer's Brook to Captain Abram Shimer's dwelling. The Captain had five or six negroes in the house at the time. Two Indians had entered before their presence was discovered. The negroes instantly rushed upon them and forced them out.

The Captain, who was in bed, aroused by the commotion, immediately ordered his slaves to barricade the windows and doors of the lower story, and to be prepared with axes to defend the house in case of an assault. While he, with the only gun they had, stationed himself at a window in the second story, after covering all but one pane with a feather bed for protection. Through this pane he fired at the Indians, who returned the fire. One ball passed through the open pane and grazed the Captain's face. One of the Indians also received a shot which broke his thigh, and he was borne off by his companions.

A small fort, situated a little above, was occupied by the militia, who had received tidings of the approach of the Indians, but thinking it false had paid no attention to it. But hearing the firing at Shimers' they hastened to the rescue. A skirmish ensued and the Indians were driven back. In their haste to recross the river they left the prisoners they had taken.

Great privation and suffering were often endured by prisoners taken by the Indians. On one occasion, shortly after the above incident, the same party of Indians captured a Mr. Patterson, when the party, who were returning to their country on the Niagara frontier, had nearly reached their destination. Being carelessly guarded one night, he escaped with two horses. After traveling two days without food he killed one of the horses. The other, becoming frightened at the scent of the blood, broke loose and ran off. In endeavoring to find him Patterson lost his way and was unable to find the spot where he killed the other animal. Thus, without horse or companion, he traveled five days guided by the sun, having nothing to eat but a snake and a toad, and such roots as he could find that were eatable. In a few days he reached the head waters of the Susquehanna. Here he used a bent pin for a hook and twisted fibres of some slippery elm bark for a line, and caught five fish, which he devoured without cooking. He then managed to construct a raft on which he floated down to the Wyoming settlements, and from thence returned back to his home in Montague.

MONTAGUE, OR "THE BRICK HOUSE."

This village is situated in the southwestern part of the township, opposite Millford, Pa.

The time of its first organization is far back, and the statements regarding it are too uncertain to fix on the exact period. It is, however, one of our oldest towns, and was originally settled by the Dutch. The place is also known as the "Brick House." It takes its name from the hotel which is built of brick, and has been occupied as a public house for several generations.

There has been a post-office here for many years, as the old stage route from Newark crossed the Delaware at this point. Here the first bridge across the Delaware was built forty years ago. This bridge although of stone, was not a substantial structure, and becoming unsafe a new wooden one was put up. This was torn down about thirteen years ago, and the present beautiful suspension bridge was constructed. The length of this bridge is 525 feet, and cost $12,500.

There are in Montague, besides the hotel, two stores and a blacksmith's shop.

MILLVILLE.

This place can hardly be called a village, it was named on account of the mills situated there. It is about a mile from Montague on the Port Jervis road, and was the scene of the Indian incursion just narrated.

The place contains one saw and two grist mills; a blacksmith's shop and a store are also here, but they are not now occupied.

REFORMED CHURCH OF MONTAGUE.

The early history of this church, known formerly as the "Minisink Church," is closely connected with the history of the "Mahacameck Church," now "Deerpark," at Port Jervis, until recently it was in the same pastoral charge, (a brief sketch of that church is given in another portion of this work.) The original building was situated in the village below the present site. The house in which the congregation now worships was built forty-three years ago; in 1868 it was renovated at a cost of $800.

NEWTON.

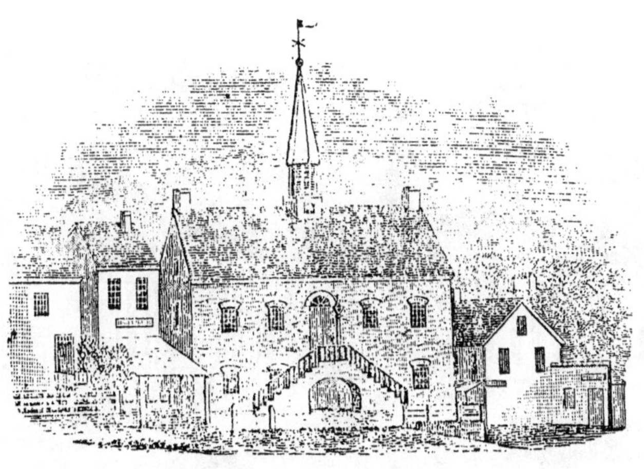

THE FIRST COURT HOUSE.

By an order of the State government in the year 1765, directing a gaol and court-house to be erected on the plantation leased by Henry Hairlocker, and within half a mile of his dwelling house, the site of the present town of Newton originally Newtown) was fixed. By this act it became the county seat.

Very shortly after, a number of dwelling houses were put up in the neighborhood of the court-house, and from that time forward there has been a steady growth in business, wealth and population.

The funds for the construction of the court-house were raised by the levying of a tax of £500 on the county in 1762, and by additional assessments in the three following years. The total cost of the building was about $5,600. The cells for the confinement of prisoners were ready in the year 1763, but the business of the courts was not commenced in the new building until two years later. In May, 1765, it was furnished and delivered to the care of the Board of Justices.

For seventy-nine years this building remained unaltered. In 1844 it was enlarged and remodeled. On the 28th of January, 1847 it took fire and was nearly destroyed. Immediate measures were taken to reconstruct it, and the present building, which is a great improvement on the former, was erected.

THE PRESENT COURT HOUSE.

The land upon which it stands, with the Public Green in front, was donated by Jonathan Hampton of Essex County. This donation of land for public use was the last of Mr. Hampton's efforts to secure the erection of the county buildings in this place, and it was mainly through his exertions that Newton and not Stillwater was selected by the Assembly as the county seat.

The first newspaper published in the county was issued in Newton on the 8th of January, 1796. It was styled *The Farmer's Journal and Newton Advertiser*, by Messrs. Elliot

Hopkins and William Husten. It was sustained for about three years only.

In 1813, a second attempt was made to start a paper here by Judge John H. Hall, which resulted in the *Sussex Register*. In 1829 the *New Jersey Herald* was established by Grant Fitch. *Sussex County Home Journal* was started in 1850 by Rev. J. L. Barlow, but within a few years was discontinued. In 1858 the first number of the *Sussex Democrat* was issued by George R. McCarter, but in 1861 it was consolidated with the *New Jersey Herald; Sussex True Democrat*, commenced in 1863 by G. D. Wallace, lived but one year, and in the fall of 1867 the first number of the *Sussex Record* appeared, edited by M. R. Hamilton. This also was sustained but a little more than a year.

The first tavern in Newton was kept by Henry Hairlocker.

The Cochran House was built in 1842 by Dennis Cochran. The Anderson House was converted into an hotel about nineteen years since. Its first proprietor was Newman E. Benjamin.

The Phillips Hotel, now a part of the Durling House, was first opened by Hezekiah Phillips and Brother about the year 1818. The Ward House was opened about the year 1820 by Janson King.

The first firm that was started in the mercantile business in this place was that of Holmes, Pemberton & Stevens. They kept a store on a lot now occupied by the upper part of the Anderson House, or the one immediately above. They commenced business in the latter part of the last century. This store was afterwards kept by David Ryerson and Garret Rosenkrans.

Fifty years ago the village contained but four hundred inhabitants and six stores.

In 1820 the principal manufactory carried on in the place was that of hats. There was a hat factory employing from ten to twenty-five hands, on Church street. It was owned by Pettit Brittin and David Kerr.

The Sussex Bank of Newton was chartered in 1818, and

for nearly fifty years David Ryerson was its President. In 1866 he was succeeded by David Thompson. At the era of the building of the Sussex Railroad, Newton took a start and grew very rapidly. The population is now about 2,300.

In the year 1870 a large public school building was erected in Newton at a cost of $35,000. It is one of the largest public schools in the State. It has an attendance of over four hundred scholars.

NEWTON COLLEGIATE INSTITUTE.

The above engraving is a fair representation of this well known Institute. It was organized April 5, 1850, and incorporated February 12, 1852, as the "Presbyterial Academy at Newton," and placed under the control of the Presbytery at Newton. For four years it continued under the direction of the Presbytery, when in the spring of 1856 the name was changed by act of Legislature to "Newton Collegiate Institute," and a boarding-house was erected at a cost of over $4,000. In the year previous to the erection of this building, the school had an attendance of 96 scholars. In 1865 the buildings were repaired. The present principal is Mr. Chester L. Teel.

THE NEWTON LIBRARY BUILDING.

This beautiful structure is built of pressed brick, 45 feet front by 75 deep, with front corners of blue limestone. It is three stories high, and a basement. It is divided lengthwise by a brick wall extending from the basement to the top of the second floor.

In the basement, the side next towards Mr. Dennis Cochran's will contain a barber shop with a series of bath rooms, back of which there will be a store room. The other side will be divided into two equal parts—the front for a store room, and the back for the library and reading-room. The first story will contain two stores. In the second story one-half will contain the library, cabinet, and reading-rooms, and the other half a room for town meetings, elections, &c., with a committee-room, and in front a spacious office. The third story extends over the whole area of the building, and will be used as a public Hall. It will seat 500 people and will contain a fine large platform, ante-rooms, and a private entrance by a rear stair-case.

The public entrance to the Hall will be in front. Over the entrance will be a neat little orchestra balcony, to be entered from the second story.

It has a Mansard roof with an ornamental tower in front. It is a beautiful building and a very valuable addition to the public conveniences and privilege of the place. It was built by a munificent donation of $25,000 from Mr. A. L. Dennis.

Its erection has been superintended by the assiduous and gratuitous care of Rev. M. Barret.

Newton also contains a foundry, a sash and blind factory, one establishment for the manufacture of agricultural implements, and two carriage manufactories, with about fifty stores. It gives employment to ten lawyers, six physicians, and as many clergymen. It contains five places of worship, Methodist, Presbyterian, Episcopal, Catholic, and Baptist. The Baptist church of which the Rev. J. T. Craig is pastor, is a small frame building, situated on the corner of Main and Liberty streets. The Methodist church is of brick, with a tower and clock. It is situated on Park Place, the Rev. Mr. Wynans is the present pastor. The Presbyterian and Episcopal churches which have recently been completed are among the finest edifices in Newton.

PRESBYTERIAN CHURCH OF NEWTON.

The first edifice was begun in the year 1786, and was four or five years building. Its dimensions were about 40 by 45 feet. It had square pews, high pulpit with sounding board. The first pastor of this church was Rev. Ira Condit. In 1827 this church was taken down and another was commenced. It was built partly on the site of the old one. It was 53 by 70 feet on the ground, and was capable of seating 600 persons. It was then the largest building in Sussex County. The minister at that time was Rev. J. L. Safer.

In the month of May, 1871, the present elegant and substantial structure was dedicated to the worship of God.

Its dimensions are 94 by 64, with a tower 20 feet square, and 54 feet high, surmounted by an elegant spire 124 feet, being a total height of 178 feet. The auditorium, with its gallery on three sides, is capable of seating one thousand persons. The present pastor is the Rev. T. L. Byington. The whole number of members is 369.

EPISCOPAL CHURCH.

The organization of the Parish of Christ's Church, Newton, dates back to the reign of George the Third in the year 1769. The first pastor of this church was the Rev. Uzal Ogden who commenced his labors in 1770. At this time there was no bishop in this country, and Mr. Ogden was obliged to go to England to receive ordination. The first parsonage to this church was built by Jonathan Hampton, Newton's great benefactor. Mr. Ogden continued his pastoral relation to this church until 1784, when he removed to Trinity Church, Newark. For thirty-six years after his departure there was a vacancy in the parish. In 1823 a new church was built on the site of the present church edifice, corner of Academy and Church streets, which was large enough to seat 250 persons. This building continued to supply the demands of the people until the year 1867, when the church, increasing in numbers and wealth, determined on the erection of the present edifice, which was built in the following year. The style is Gothic, built of the native blue limestone of this region. The spire is 108 feet high, surmounted by a cross 12 feet long. The cost of the building was about $25,000, and in point of beauty and durableness is in advance of many churches costing double this amount. *The Catholic church* is a fine brick building, it has only recently been completed.

SANDYSTON TOWNSHIP.

The township of Sandyston was erected by Royal Patent from Wallpack in the year 1762. It is bounded north by Montague, south by Wallpack, east by Frankford and west by the Delaware, having an average length of seven and a quarter miles and a width of six. The township is well watered throughout by the Little and Big Flat Brook flowing through the centre, and forming a junction about a mile southeast of Peter's Valley, uniting with the Delaware at the southern extremity of Wallpack. The post-offices of this township are Hainesville, Laytons, Bevans, and Tuttle's Corner.

HAINESVILLE.

Hainesville is situated in the northren part of the township, on the "Little Flatbrook." The village is about a mile in length, extending along the Stage Road to Port Jervis, N. Y. It has only recently received the name of Hainesville, which was given to it in honor of Ex-Gov. Haines of this county. The place was previously known by the name of Sandyston. It was made a post village in 1825, previous to that time a tavern and two or three houses were all that was here; but in that year Parshall Howell built the hotel now standing, also one or two other houses, a store was also built. The mail was then brought twice a week on a four-horse stage which ran from Newark to Montrose, N. Y. It was run night and day, stopping in this county at White Hall, Newton, Augusta, Tuttle's Corner, Sandyston, and Brick House. Hainesville has the honor of being the birthplace of Simon Courtright. When a young man he emigrated to Virginia, but returned after a short stay and settled on a farm in this neighborhood. Soon after his return he was elected Justice of the Peace, and afterwards served three terms in the Legislature, he was for fifteen years a Judge in the county. There are three stores and an hotel, a blacksmith's, wheelwright's, cooper's, and undertaker's shop here. For some time past there has been little, if any, increase in the population.

HAINESVILLE CHURCH.

In 1855 a contract was given for a church in Hainesville. It was built in the same year on land deeded to "The Reformed Church" with the condition that any other orthodox denomination should have the right to worship in it, when it was not occupied by them. By this provision the Methodists have regularly held service here. The building only cost $800 and is an outpost of the Minisink church in Montague. The first preacher was Rev. David A. Jones, who preached alternately in Montague and here.

The Methodist brethren are now discussing the question of building a church for themselves. They cherish the hope that the difficulties which delay their action will soon be removed.

LAYTONS, OR CENTREVILLE.

Laytons, known also as Centreville, was named nearly a half century ago, from John Layton, who for some time kept the hotel. About thirty years since the hotel changed hands and the party occupying it attempted to change its name to Centreville. In 1861 a post-office was established here with the old name of Laytons which re-established the name. The village is very beautiful, situated on the Little Flatbrook in the Minisink Valley, two miles from the Delaware, lying about midway between Hainesville and Peter's Valley. It contains an hotel, one store, one blacksmith's, one wheelwright's, and one cabinetmaker's shop. The church here called "Laytons Methodist Church" was built about the year 1830. It has since been rebuilt, services are held regularly. No record of this church could be found.

PETER'S VALLEY.

Peter's Valley, or "The Corners," as it is called, was named nearly a hundred years ago from Peter Vanness. It is situated in the lower part of the township. The hotel is one of the oldest buildings in the place, it was originally built for a school house, and religious services were performed in it on the Sabbath. It was a building one and a half stories high, afterwards raised to two. It is now occupied as an hotel. The scenery from the hills surrounding the town is not surpassed by any in our county. A post office has been recently placed here called "Bevans P. O." There is in the place a store, a blacksmith's shop, and two coopers' shops, besides the hotel.

PETER'S VALLEY REFORMED CHURCH.

The Reformed Church at Peter's Valley was built in the year 1840, on land that was deeded to it by Alpheus Gustin and wife, in the year 1838. The building cost $14,000. It was repaired in 1865. This church, together with those at Bushkill, Wallpack and Dingman's are at present under the charge of Rev. G. S. Garrison and Rev. John F. Shaw.

A small church built since the "Reformed" is occupied by the Universalists.

TUTTLE'S CORNER.

Tuttle's Corner can hardly be called a village. The hotel, where the mail is received, and a few houses being all the buildings it contains. There has been a postoffice here for many years. Previous to its establishment the mail was brought from Newton by the farmers themselves, each one taking his turn. It received its name from the first Postmaster of the place.

It is situated about four and a half miles from Branchville on the old stage road.

SPARTA TOWNSHIP.

This township is about eight miles in width and about the same in length. It is bounded north by Hardyston, south by Byram, east by Morris county, and west by Andover and Lafayette. In the northern part of this township is a vein of zinc ore extending four miles. The Wallkill, which rises in the Northern part of Byram, flows directly through the centre of the township. A more beautiful valley is not to be found in the county than that through which the stream here flows. The surface of this township is mountainous. The great mineral wealth of this district attracts a large population of miners.

The villages are Sparta, Ogdensburg and Sussex Mills.

SPARTA.

Sparta is situated upon the Wallkill, a little south of the centre of the township, eight miles southeast of Newton, and three miles south of Ogdensburg. It is built on the highest land in the State. Within a short distance of this village the Paulinskill takes its rise. The place was settled in about the year 1770, but for many years its growth was slow. Its population, however, has increased within the past forty years, threefold. For many years there was a female academy in this place, but for the past few years it has not been opened.

At one time an immense amount of iron was forged in the village. Six forges were kept constantly employed; the ruins of five of these are to be found here at the present time. A large number of anchors were annually manufactured here; the Ogden mine supplied most of the ore.

There are now here two hotels, four or five general stores, two grist and one saw mill, an apothecary, two or three blacksmith shops, a wheelwright and a cooper's shop. It has a population of about 300.

PRESBYTERIAN CHURCH OF SPARTA.

This is one of the oldest churches in this section. The first building was erected in the year 1786. This church was the first to avail itself of the act passed by the Legislature of the State in that year, which provided for the incorporation of religious bodies. Lord Rutherford, a Scotch nobleman, donated to this church fifty acres of land, upon a portion of which the present building stands.

Previous to the erection of the church, services are said to have been held here in a log hut.

The first pastor was the Rev. H. W. Hunt. The building has been repaired twice since it was first erected; once in 1837 at a cost of $1,156, and in 1869 the ceiling was raised and beautifully frescoed; this, with other improvements and repairs cost over $4,000. It has now 109 members. The present pastor is the Rev. Wm. B. McKee.

M. E. CHURCH.

The first building was put up in 1837; Rev. Sedgwick Russling was the pastor. This building stood near where a wheelwright shop now stands, on the main street.

In 1868 the present fine structure was completed; it is situated on the Newton road, a little west of the village. The Rev. W. B. Wigg is pastor.

OGDENSBURG

Robert Ogden, from whom the village takes its name, removed from Elizabethtown to this locality in the year 1765 or 66. He was the father of the noted Aaron Ogden, who commanded the famous Life Guards, of General Washington.

There were some persons living near the site of the village before the time of Ogden: Among them were the Hoaglands and Wades. The growth of the place has not been rapid, and the number of buildings is still quite small; outside of its mining operations little business is done.

But the Midland Railroad now passes through it, this, combined with the rapid increase of the work at the mines, with other attractions have given it an impulse never before known, and inspired its citizens with courage and hope. It now promises to take place among the most prosperous of our business towns.

SUSSEX MILLS.

Sussex Mill is situated in the western part of this township. It has only recently received its present name. About eight years since a rich vein of lead ore was supposed to have been discovered on the site of this place, then known as Howellsville. The property was bought by the Sussex Lead Company, and a considerable amount of money was spent in opening it up. But the vein being soon exhausted it was abandoned, and the place for five years remained unimproved. About two years since Mr. Benjamin H. Wright bought the property and changed the name to Sussex Mills. Since that time he has built a mill for grinding fertilizers, a saw mill and a grist mill. The latter was built the present summer, and will probably be in operation soon.

STILLWATER TOWNSHIP.

This township is contiguous to Warren County, which forms its southern border. It is wedge-shaped, its apex pointing duc north towards Sandyston. The Blue mountains on the west separate it from Wallpack. It has Hampton and Green on the east and southeast. 1ts extreme length from north to south is ten miles, and its greatest width six and a half.

Originally it was included in Hardwick, but in the year 1824, when Warren County was erected, it was made a separate township and received its present name. Its surface is throughout uneven, and in some parts rough and mountainous but the land is fertile, and well suited for the raising of all kinds of grain and farm produce. *Swartswood Pond*, near the centre of the township is a beautiful sheet of water about three miles long by one wide. It was first called Swartwout's from a man of that name who had a farm near by. At the time of the French and Indian wars this man was brutally tortured to death by the Indians. Besides this large pond there are numerous smaller ones. These together with the Paulinskill river and its tributaries abundantly water this township.

The villages are Stillwater, Fredon,* Middleville, Swartswood, and a cluster of houses in the southwestern corner of the township named Gratitude.

STILLWATER.

The site of the present village of Stillwater was bought and first settled by John P. Burnhardt and Casper Shafer, in the year 1742; after them came the Wintermutes, Mains, Staleys and others, principally Germans, who settled in the valley of the Paulinskill, some of whom afterwards moved off into other sections of the country. Mr. Shafer erected the first mill at this place, and as it was the only mill for many miles around, it was resorted to from far and near.

The difficulties which attended the getting of their grain to mill were very great, as the roads were simply paths through a continuous forest. Wagons were not then used. The grain was brought on horses led over the mountains, for many miles; and the flour carried back in the same way. This mill was at first very simple in its construction, and could only grind four or five bushels a day. As the business increased a large one was erected, after which flour ground here was shipped down the Paulinskill to the Delaware, and thence to Philadelphia. But the construction of other mills below on the Paulinskill soon cut it off from this source of trade.

A German church was erected here in 1771 on ground set apart for it, and for a cemetery, a number of years before, by Mr. Burnhardt one of the first persons buried in this cemetery. In 1775 a fulling mill was erected here by Peter Wintermute, about a half a mile below the village.

At one time Stillwater was seriously talked of as the most suitable place for the county seat and for the erection of the county buildings, but Newton was finally decided upon, at the present time there is in the place a large grist mill, one or two stores, an hotel, a Presbyterian church, a Methodist church, and fifteen or twenty dwellings. Stillwater wants the facilities of a railroad to make it a thriving village.

STILLWATER PRESBYTERIAN CHURCH.

The first church erected in what is now Stillwater Township, was a stone building about 35 by 40 feet with galleries on three sides, bearing date 1771. It was a Union enterprise. One branch was of German Lutherans, and the other of German Calvinists. These constituted the church. They do not appear ever to have had a pastor, but were supplied with occasional preaching until 1816, when they were taken under the care of the Classis of New Brunswick, and supplied till 1823, when they were transferred to the Presbytery of Newton. The present church edifice was erected in the year 1838. Size, 36 by 45 feet; with 20 feet front pillars, and a gallery on three sides, at a cost of $2,200. The parsonage, one and a half stories high, twenty-six feet front, by some fifty deep, cost about $2,000. The present pastor Rev. T. B. Condit, after about two years labor was installed in June, 1839.

FREDON

Is a post village situated in the southeastern corner of the township. The short low range of hills which separates this township from Green, lies just to the east of this village. It is on the stage road from Newton to Blairstown in Warren County, about four miles from the former place. The stage and mail route from Newton to Flatbrookville also passes through Fredon.

The "Fountain House" here is a fine, large, well-furnished hotel.

The church is used during the week for a school. The attendance on the Sabbath is always very large.

The population of Fredon is about 150.

MIDDLEVILLE.

This place, about two miles north of Stillwater, is a small post village of about twenty or thirty inhabitants. It contains an hotel and store, and a good-sized building which has been leased at various times for different mechanical purposes.

It is situated on a branch of the Paulinskill, half a mile from Swartswood Pond.

SWARTSWOOD.

Swartswood or Paterson, as it *was* called, is on the northwest boundary of Swartswood Pond, near the line which separates this township from Hampton. It contains a store, a cooper and two blacksmith shops, an hotel and a saw-mill. There are also here two churches—Methodist and Presbyterian.

During the summer months pleasure and fishing boats are in constant demand on the pond by parties visiting the place.

SWARTSWOOD PRESBYTERIAN CHURCH.

In the year 1833 a house was dedicated and a congregation organized known as the Second Presbyterian Church of Stillwater. It was placed two and a half miles northwest of the present building. Owing to the unfavorable locality the building has been abandoned and the congregation dissolved. The present church edifice was erected in 1855, size 32x42 at a cost of $2,250. It was organized in December, 1853, by a committee from Newton Presbytery. It has had no pastor but has been chiefly supplied by Rev. T. B. Condit.

VERNON TOWNSHIP.

This township is situated in the northeast of the county bounded north by Orange County, N. Y., south by Hardyston, east by Passaic County, and west by Wantage. The surface is mountainous. The Wawayanda range on the east, with the Wallkill and Pochunk Mountains cover the greater portion of the township. The Wallkill river with its tributary streams, the Wawayanda Lake and several small ponds besides numerous creeks water the township throughout. There are also on the summit of some of these mountains small lakes, which is one of the many curious phenomena of this region. Near the southwest portion of this township commences the tract of marshy land known as the "drowned lands of the Wallkill." It is quite narrow until it enters the State of New York, where it extends five miles in width.

Although many attempts have been and still are made to drain this marsh, they have not yet been successful. But wherever portions of it have been drained the soil is found to be a rich vegetable mould.

The scenery from the farm of Mr. Jacob V. Little, on the top of the Pochunk, overlooking the Kitanny Valley, lying between this mountain and the Blue Mountains on the west, is truly beautiful. This great valley, which extends far into Wantage, is not a level surface, but traversed from north to south by several ridges of low hills, with meadow lands of considerable width between. The view also from this mountain extends north to the Catskill and south as far as the Delaware Water Gap, a distance of seventy-five miles.

VERNON.

This village is situated in about the centre of the township, and is the principal place. It lies just to the west of the Wawayanda Mountains on a small creek. It contains three stores, two blacksmith shops, two wheelwright shops, a grist-mill and two cheese factories. The population is about 200.

The corner stone of the Methodist Episcopal church at this place was laid on the 21st of September, 1871, and the building was completed this year at a cost of $8,000. This is a beautiful frame building 38x70 feet. There is also an Episcopal church at Vernon.

MCAFFEE'S VALLEY

Is situated in the southwestern part of Vernon on the Black Creek. It was called West Vernon until recently. The name was changed when the postoffice was established on account of its similarity to other names in the State.

A branch railroad has just been completed from the Midland to this place to carry off the iron ores from the mine near by. The place contains an hotel and a small store.

CANISTEER.

Canisteer is situated in the extreme south-east corner of the township. A large forge was for many years in constant use here, and a fine water power was sustained by a series of artificial ponds to the north of the village. But little is now done here. A mine of iron ore has been recently opened on lands which were owned by Mr. Adam Smith, but is not being worked at present.

CANISTEER M. E. CHURCH.

This church was built in about the year 1857 by Mr. Adam Smith of Canisteer. The first pastor was Rev. Joshua Burch. Since the time of its erection it has been closed a year, but with this exception it has sustained regular preaching. The present pastor is the Rev. Daniel H. Leith.

WAWAYANDA

Is a small place near Wawayanda Lake, known also as Double Pond. It contains a store, an old forge, a furnace, and a few dwelling houses. The lake, which is about two miles long, and near which this place stands, is a most beautiful sheet of water. It is situated in the northeastern part of the township.

Several small mines have been opened in this vicinity, but little is being done in them at present.

GLENWOOD, OR NORTH VERNON.

Is situated in the northwestern portion of the township on a small creek. The name was changed from North Vernon to Glenwood at the time it was made a post village for the same reason that changed the name of West Vernon to McAffee's Valley.

WALLPACK TOWNSHIP.

The township of Wallpack lies in the southwestern extremity of the county, bounded north by Sandyston, south by Warren County, east by Stillwater, and west by the Delaware River. The Delaware in the southwest corner sweeps around a large bend and flows back about a mile in the opposite direction nearly to Flatbrookville, where it makes a short bend and returns. The eastern portion of the township is mountainous and very thinly inhabited. The population is scattered through the centre, along the Flatbrook, which flows through a most beautiful valley.

From Stillwater it is separated by the Blue Mountains. The line separating Wallpack from Sandyston is a part of the division line which separated what in our father's time was called East and West Jersey. Flatbrookville and Wallpack Centre are the only villages in the township.

FLATBROOKVILLE.

This village is situated on the west bank of the Flatbrook, near its mouth, where it empties into the Delaware. It is hemmed in on all sides by the Blue Mountain range, which cuts it off from the constant communication with the county seat which is enjoyed by other small towns.

It has been built up in the last fifty years, previous to which a saw-mill only marked the place. This mill has gone through many changes; at first it was built of logs, with the cumbrous old gearing of that period. At the present time we find there a large frame building with modern improvements in machinery to utilize the water power, which is most excellent at this place. A mail route and stage line is established between this place and Newton, running three times a week and returning the same day. There is also a mail route on Saturday of each week between this place and Layton's in Sandyston, stopping also at Wallpack Centre. There are two good stores, a wagon manufactory and an hotel here. Flatbrookville is beautifully located. The Delaware, making the graceful sweep around the mountain before referred to, doubles its track with a shorter curve, and then bears away to the south along the base of the mountain. From many points on these mountains, the eye traverses a range of mountain scenery from fifty to sixty miles in extent. This vast landscape is continuously intermingled with woodlands and flourishing fields.

FLATBROOKVILLE (REFORMED) CHURCH.

This is one of the oldest churches in the county. It dates back to 1737, and is one of the four Reformed churches on the Delaware, of which Johannes Casparus Freyenmoet was pastor, of which mention is made in the sketch of the Mahackameck Church. In 1793 it was incorporated as the Reformed Dutch Church of Wallpack, which name it retained until 1860, when a geographical division was made, dividing this township into Upper and Lower Wallpack, placing this congregation with that of the church at Bushkill, Pa., and since known as the Reformed Dutch Church of Lower Wallpack. In 1855 the present church edifice was erected at a cost of $1,400. The present pastor is the Rev. John Fletcher Shaw.

WALLPACK CENTRE.

This is a small post village in the northern portion of the township, situated on the Flatbrook. It contains a store, a blacksmith shop and a Methodist church. Part of the blacksmith shop now standing here was once a portion of an old school-house then known as Myres' School-house. In form it was an octagon, and in its day was quite celebrated. Until about twenty years since the locality was known by this name. About a mile west of the village, on the Delaware, there was once an old fort, and near this spot for many years there stood a church, long since removed.

WALLPACK CENTRE M. E. CHURCH.

This church, together with the church at Dingman's Ferry, is now under the charge of Rev. John F. Shaw. The corner stone of this edifice was laid in June, 1871, on land donated by Jacob Roe. It is a frame building with brick foundations and a slate roof. It is 60x38 feet, and will seat 300 persons. The audience room, 20 feet from floor to ceiling, is handsomely painted and frescoed. This elegant structure, which took the place of a quaint old meeting-house, a relic of primitive days, was dedicated in March, 1872, and on the day of its dedication $1,500 was raised by subscription to pay off the debt.

WANTAGE TOWNSHIP.

Wantage is about eleven miles long and about seven broad. It is the largest township in the county, having an area of over 40,000 square acres. It is bounded north by Orange County, N. Y., south by Frankford, Lafayette and Hardyston, east by Vernon and Hardyston, which are separated from it by the Wallkill, and west by Montague.

Wantage comprises that portion of the Kittanny Valley which lies between Pochunk Mountain on the east, and the Blue Mountains on the west.

The surface of this valley is uneven, covered with several ridges of low hills, running north and south, with bottoms of considerable width, in which is land of great fertility, Along these valleys run two small streams, tributaries of the Wallkill.

The natural scenery of this region is rarely surpassed. It is thickly settled throughout, and contains about a sixth of the whole population of the county. Less than one hundred and fifty years ago the Indians claimed the whole of the district as their hunting grounds, where now villages and farm houses thickly dot the surface. The early settlers of Wantage are of a mixed origin, some of German and others of New England parentage, besides Huguenots, or French Protestants. These latter, exiled from Holland in the latter part of the seventeenth century, emigated to America, and passing up the Hudson, settled near Kingston, N. Y., from which place some individuals pushed farther on and settled in this town.

The villages in this township are Deckertown, Beemerville, Coleville, Libertyville, Mt. Salem and Rockport.

DECKERTOWN.

About the year 1740 Peter Decker, a Hollander, the great grandfather of John B. Decker, and ancestor of almost all who bear that name still living in the township, passed over the Blue Mountains from the Neversink settlement, and came into this valley. Being struck with the exceeding fertility of the soil, he immediately prepared to erect a dwelling, and selected for its site the spot on which Deckertown now stands. His house stood near Gilbert Chardevoyne's Hotel. This was probably the first white man's abode in the township.

The village of Deckertown is situated about fifteen miles northeast from Newton on the Clove river. It is the business centre and principal place for trade to a district ten miles in extent. Since the construction of the Midland Railroad the village has taken a new start. Several new and handsome buildings have been erected.

Two or three large and well-furnished hotels provide ample and comfortable accommodations for travelers.

A newspaper called the *Deckertown Independent* was commenced in the spring of 1870 by Stephen H. Sayer, which is still published under the able management of Messrs. Sayer & Noble.

No school of any note had been sustained in the township until 1833, when William Rankin commenced an academy in this village under great difficulties, not for want of personal merit, however, as was afterwards proved, but for want of an appreciation among the people of such an institution. By persistent energy, however, he built up for himself quite a reputation, so that ten years afterward, in 1843, an article appeared in the *Sussex Register* which spoke of his success and qualifications, and stated that about a thousand youth had been under his charge and that many of his pupils had become prepared to enter college, or commence professional studies.

There is now situated here a well-built academy ably conducted.

There are also about fifteen stores, a large grist-mill, a blacksmith's shop, and a foundry running a ten horse-power engine.

BEEMERVILLE

Is situated in the southwestern portion of this township, at the base of the Blue Mountain range. It is divided into what is often called Upper and Lower Beemerville; the latter is about a mile southeast of the other, and contains a saw-mill and store; it is on a branch of the Papakating River. Upper Beemerville contains two carriage manufactories an hotel, a tannery, store, and harness shop, two blacksmiths and one wheelwright.

It received its name about fifty years ago from Henry Beemer, who kept the hotel here at that time.

A cemetery was laid out here in 1866, and called the "Beemerville Cemetery." It contains five acres of land, having a good osage hedge around it.

The population of Beemerville is about 200. It has long had the promise of a railroad to run through Culver's Gap, connecting it with places east and west. The nearest station now is Deckertown, five and a half miles distant on the Midland Railroad.

The Clove Church, in Clove Valley, and the Deckertown and Beemerville Presbyterian Churches were for many years under one charge, the notices of them are, therefore, given under the head of

CLOVE CHURCH.

In the year 1787 a Reformed church was organized and a church named Clove Church, from the valley in which it was built, the first pastor being the Rev. Elias Van Benschotten. This church was for many years in a very flourishing state, but after the death of Mr. Van Benschotten it was neglected by its own denomination, and in 1817 it was made the First Presbyterian Church of Wantage, organized by Rev. Gershom Williams, of the Presbytery of Jersey. About this time the

PRESBYTERIAN CHURCH OF DECKERTOWN

was built, and Mr. Williams preached here as well as at the Clove, and at the "Log Meeting House" for a year and a half as a stated supply.

In June, 1829, the Clove Church was taken down and a new meeting house built, which cost $3,300.

The "Old Log Meeting House" was situated at Beemerville, under the same charge with the Clove and Deckertown churches. The Presbyterian members of this church, however, wishing to organize separately, they determined to build a new church, the "Log Meeting House" being occupied by Presbyterians, Baptists and Congregationalists in common. The new church was of stone. It was built in 1835, at a cost of $3,000, and called the Second Presbyterian Church of Wantage.

Rev. Andrew Tully, the present minister, was the first installed pastor of this church.

"OLD LOG MEETING HOUSE," BEEMERVILLE.

This building was torn down in about the year 1823, when a frame building was erected as a free church. At this time the Congregationalists were the most numerous denomination; that, together with the Presbyterians and Baptists worshiped in this church. In 1835, when the Presbyterian church was built the Congregationalists joined them. The union church from that period went down, and for several years past has been unoccupied.

COLEVILLE.

This village is situated in the western portion of this township, at the base of the Blue Mountains. It contains a saw-mill and two grist-mills, driven by a stream which takes its rise at Sand Pond on the mountain back of the place. There are also two stores, a blacksmith's and a wheelwright's shop, a harness-maker's shop, a cheese-box manufactory, and two hotels. The Dotterer House is a first-class hotel. A fine hall is attached to this building, where ample accommodation for entertainments of every description is furnished.

LIBERTYVILLE

Is a post village about three miles south of Coleville; contains a store, a blacksmith shop, and a Methodist church.

The old Patterson stage route ran through this place and was the means of establishing a post-office here. This road was established in about the year 1830, and passed through Snufftown, Hamburgh, Deckertown, Libertyville and Montague, in this county.

COLEVILLE AND LIBERTYVILLE M. E. CHURCHES.

These two Methodist churches are in one charge. The Red Church, called so on account of that being the original color of the building, was erected in 1837, by Isaiah Winfield. The first pastor of this church was the Rev. Mr. Baker.

The Libertyville M. E. Church was organized in 1860, and the building was immediately put up. The pastor in charge at this time being Rev. S. C. Mertene. The ground upon which the church edifice stands was deeded to it by Jacob Courtwright.

Rev. W. McCain is now on the charge of these two churches.

MT. SALEM.

This is a small village in the northern extremity of the township. It contains a store, blacksmith's and a wheelwright's shop, an hotel and a still-house. There are two Baptist churches here, neither of which are regulary occupied.

ROCKPORT, a short distance from this place, contains a blacksmith's and a wheelwright's shop.

MAHACKAMECK DUTCH REFORMED CHURCH, NOW DEERPARK REFORMED CHURCH, PORT JERVIS, N. Y., AND ASSOCIATE REFORMED CHURCHES ON THE DELAWARE.

The Mahackameck Dutch Reformed Church was organized in the year 1737. Being then without a regular pastor this church and three others on the Delaware selected a lad, Johannes Casparus Fryenmoet, who had begun to study for the ministry, and sent him to Holland to complete his education and receive ordination.

He returned in 1741. His charge consisted of the four churches on the Delaware—the Mahackameck at Port Jervis, the Minisink at Montague, Wallpack Church in Wallpack, and Smithfield Church at Smithfield, Pa. The salary paid by the four churches amounted to $400.

Mr. Fryenmoet continued his labors in this field until 1756. In September, 1760, Rev. Thomas Romeyne commenced his labors as pastor, and continued until the year 1772. From this time until 1785, a period of thirteen years, the churches were not regularly supplied, owing probably to the troubled state of the country during the Revolutionary war.

On the 11th of May, 1785, a call was given by the Mahackameck, Minisink and Wallpack churches to Rev. Elias Van Benschoten, who accepted it and was duly installed in the August following. He continued as pastor until 1800.

The next regular pastor was the Rev. John Demorest, who was with them for five years.

For eight years afterward the churches were filled by occasional supplies, when, in 1816, Rev. Cornelius C. Elting accepted a call from this and the Minisink churches. He continued as their pastor for twenty-one years, after which his services were exclusively given to the Mahackameck church.

As this last act broke the link which connected the Mahackmeck church with those in this county, it is not the intention to continue its history; it might, however, be well to state that the Mahackameck Church, now Deerpark, has recently completed a fine building at a cost of about $50,000, and is now in a very flourishing condition.

A description of the present buildings of the Minisink and Wallpack churches will be found in the description of the villages in which they are situated.

A DESCRIPTIVE SKETCH

OF THE

PRINCIPAL MINERALS AND MINES

FOUND IN

SUSSEX COUNTY.

COMPILED FROM THE REPORT OF A LATE SURVEY BY THE STATE GEOLOGIST.

The mineral wealth of this mountain region early attracted the attention of settlers, and the working of iron mines was begun about the year 1700.

The most important minerals found in the mountains of this county are Limestone, Hudson River Slate, Iron and Zinc.

LIMESTONE.

There are found two kinds of limestone—magnesian and fossiliferous. At Roseville there is an outcrop of blue limestone of magnesian formation, and north of the Roseville mine, near the Andover road, are two separate hills of brownish-red arenaceous limestone. Between Franklin Furnace and Sparta there are several outcrops. The rock forms little knolls, and irregular ridges of considerable height, separated by smooth meadows or flats of the valley. Beginning again at McAffee's Valley, the eastern portion is underlaid by blue limestone that runs north to the State line and beyond into Warwick Valley. The Hamburg and Wawayanda Mountains limit it on the east, on the west it joins the crystalline limestone.

The Valley of the Paulinskill is a long limestone valley extending from near Branchville to the Delaware. It is bounded on all sides by slate.

About two miles northwest of Middleville, on the farm of Joseph Huff, and near the stream, is a quarry of this rock in the midst of a slate country. The rock here is compact, blue in color, and thick bedded.

Fossiliferous limestone is the name locally applied to a limestone lying between the magnesian and the Hudson River slate. This limestone can be traced by its various outcroppings from Belvidere in Warren County to Frankford Township, appearing in this county at the following points: West of Stillwater there is a hill of it; the road from Stillwater to Millbrook crosses it. At Phillips' saw-mill, one mile north of Huntsville, it is found adjoining the slate; there is another about one mile northeast of this locality very similar in the position and character of the rock; the next appearance is southeast of Newton on the farm of Col. William Babbitt, and another on the farm of Mr. Jesse G. Roe, half a mile east-northeast of Branchville. It is on the southern brow of a high hill, the summit of which is slate.

HUDSON RIVER SLATE.

This is a rock like that which is found along the Hudson River. Hence its name.

The most perfect form of it is soft and free from grit, and possesses the property of cleavage or splitting up into slates to a wonderful degree.

Near the State line north of Deckertown, at the quarries of Asa Carr, the stone is remarkable for its even beds and for showing no cleavage.

There are two large outcrops in Sussex County. The largest of these is the long narrow ridge that runs from Springdale northeast by the Paulinskill Meadows, east of Lafayette, west of Monroe Corners and terminates in Hardyston Township near the Wantage line.

Separated from this by a short interval of limestone along

the Newton and Andover road, the slate again appears in several places, nearly to Johnsonburg in Warren County. An exposure of slate is also found on the road to Greensville near the bridge, over a branch of the Pequest, and the smooth surface indicates a continuous outcrop. Near J. P. Stackhouse's place in Greensville is a limited outcrop of slate in the midst of the limestone.

About one mile northwest of Swartswood there is an old slate quarry, worked a little several years ago. It is close to the stream of Long Pond. There is but little drift or top-dirt.

About one and a half miles southwest of Newton is Van Sickles slate quarry. The excavation may be twenty-five feet deep.

Near Lafayette is the only other quarry in this county worked to any extent; it is about a mile north of the village; it has been opened twenty-eight years.

Flagstone is the name given to thin-bedded rocks of any age used for flagstones. The only locality in the county where these are quarried is on Flagstone Hill, three miles north of Deckertown. The thickness of the beds is from one to six inches. Some stones of enormous dimensions have been quarried from this place.

MAGNETIC IRON ORES.

This ore is known to mineralogists under the name of Magnetite and Magnetic Iron ore, and to chemists as Magnetic, or Black Oxide of Iron. It consists, when pure, of 74.4 per cent. of iron, 27.6 per cent. of oxygen. It is attracted by the magnet, though not always itself magnetic.

As an ore it is always found mixed with more or less rock, the rock being sometimes in grains, and at other times in large masses or in stratified streaks. Iron pyrites are found in minute quantity in many of the ores, and in some places so much is found as to render the ore unfit for the present modes of working.

LIST OF MINES OF MAGNETIC IRON ORE IN SUSSEX COUNTY.

	Mine	Township	
1	Silver Mine	Byram	Township
2	Stanhope or Hude Mine	"	"
3	Haggerty Mine	"	"
4	Roseville Mine	"	"
5	Glendon Mine	Green	"
6	Ogden Mine	Sparta	"
7	Green Mine, Wawayanda Mts	Vernon	"
8	Wawayanda Mines	"	"
9	Green Mine, Pochuck Mt	"	"
10	Bird Mine, Pochuck Mt	"	"
11	Franklin Mines, Franklin Furnace	Hardyston	"
12	Andover Mine	Andover	"
13	Tar Hill Mine	"	"

DESCRIPTION OF IRON MINES.

1. Silver Mine.—This locality is upon the Sussex Railroad between Andover and its terminus at Waterloo, two or three miles below the former place. The principal opening is two hundred yards or so west of the railroad. A large proportion of this ore (34.4) is sulphur. The place, though small in extent, is of interest from the peculiar character of the seam of ore, which is of considerable size, although from its great irregularity no distinct idea as to its width could be arrived at.

2. Stanhope or Hude Mine.—This mine is situated about a mile north of Stanhope. The first workings made here were by Mr. Jonathan Dickerson, about the year 1802; these are now filled in. The ore taken out at that time was smelted at the Lockwood Forge, and the iron was made into scythes, and was considered very suitable for this purpose. Some ten years since Mr. Edwin Post made an opening 25 to 30 feet deep about 350 yards south-southwest of the old mine, and took out several hundred tons of ore, when it was abandoned on account of the vast amount of pyrites.

3. Haggerty Mine.—This mine is one mile and a quarter northeast of Stanhope, near the road leading from that place

to Lake Hopatcong. A considerable quantity of ore is said to have been obtained here.

4. Roseville Mine—Is situated between three and four miles southeast of Andover. It was worked at intervals for several years by the Trenton Iron Company, when in 1868 it passed into the hands of the Andover Iron Company, lying idle at present. There are two principal openings, at each of which a very considerable mass of ore has been extracted. The mine is nearly eight hundred feet long and fifty feet deep.

5. Glendon or Chapin Mine—Is in Green Township, one mile southwest of Andover. The mine is located just at the junction of the white limestone and gneiss. This ore contained such a large proportion of garnet that it was called garnet ore.

6. Ogden Mine—Is situated about two miles southeast of Ogdensburg, in Sparta Township. The first of these mines was opened in 1772, and it has been worked at intervals ever since, though on account of its remoteness from market it was not worked with the vigor that its magnitude would have warranted. The opening of the Ogden Mine Railroad to Lake Hopatcong and the Morris Canal has furnished an outlet for these rich mines, and have since been worked with great vigor by the Roberts, Glendon and Stanhope Iron Companies.

7. Green Mine—In Vernon Township, on the Wawayanda Mountain, one-half mile from the State line. A good many successful openings have been made into this mine, and large quantities of ore have been taken out.

8. Wawayanda Mine—Is in Vernon Township, immediately north of the last mine. The ore does not occur in regular veins, but in irregular deposits, and their thickness is exceedingly variable, but the general direction is in a straight course. The mine has been lying idle for many years.

9. Green, or Copperas Mine, Pochuck Mt.—Is in Vernon

Township on the east slope of the mountain, one mile and a half northeast of McAffee's Valley. It is mentioned by Dr. Kitchell in the report of 1855, that, "at the copperas works, near Decker's Pond, . . . iron pyrites constitute the greater portion of a stratum of rock which was worked forty years ago to a considerable extent for the purpose of manufacturing copperas from the ore." The mine remained idle for about sixty years, but it is now successfully worked, and by the track that has been recently laid from the Midland Railroad, the ore is brought directly into market.

10. BIRD MINE---Is four miles north of the last, and on the west slope of the same mountain.

11. FRANKLIN MINES—Are in Hardyston Township, near Franklin Furnace. On the hill south of the old furnace there are several places where magnetic iron ore has been raised in quantities. The ore is hard, firm and quite rich. The furnaces building at Franklin Furnace, for smelting the ore, are among the largest in this country. It is said that they will require 100,000 tons of coal every year, from Scranton, to smelt the iron, and the same cars will return with the same quantity of iron to mix with the Pennsylvania ores, and make a better grade of iron than could be made without it.

12. ANDOVER MINE—Is about one and a half miles north of the village of Andover. It has been extensively worked by the Trenton Iron Company, but is now owned by the Andover Iron Company. The color of the magnetic iron ore here is black, inclined to blue. There are at least twenty-four separate and distinct minerals found at this mine and in its immediate vicinity, among which are found in large numbers garnet crystals, sometimes several inches in diameter, of chocolate-brown and wine-red colors, amorphous malachite, and translucent green feldspar.

13. TAR HILL MINE—Is in the same vicinity; there are two large openings made here. It has been worked at various times, and has yielded large quantities of ore.

HEMATITES IRON ORE.

This ore, when pure, has a metallic appearance, is of various shades of color, and is composed of 70 metallic iron and 30 oxygen in 100 parts. It is easily distinguished from other ores of iron by its reddish streak and powder. A great part of the iron manufactured in different countries is from this ore, and although it requires much more heat to smelt than other ores, it produces an iron of excellent quality.

SIMPSON MINE—Is in Vernon Township and two and a half miles northeast of Hamburgh. Excavations have been made to a considerable depth, and large quantities of ore have been removed and smelted in the old Hamburgh Furnace, yielding an iron of superior quality. A large proportion of it is quite pure and almost entirely free from foreign materials.

THE POCHUCK AND EDSALL MINES in this vicinity are of the same general character as the last, and both have yielded well.

ZINC ORES.

There are two localities in the State where ores of zinc have been found in workable quantities, both of which are in this county. One is at Sterling Hill near Ogdensburg, worked by the Passaic Zinc Company, and the other on Mine Hill, at Franklin Furnace, by the New Jersey Zinc Company. The process of separating these ores is as follows: The lumps of ore passing between two solid iron wheels are crushed and then washed in two revolving cylinders, thus drawn up into troughs and carried into tubs, where the ore, by a simple process, is separated from the limestone and base material; the former being heavier sinks to the bottom and the latter is carried off by the water.

Four years ago the zinc mines of Sussex County were said to supply 25,000 tons of ore a year, which was manufactured into white oxide and spelter, yielding 7,000 tons of the oxide and 500 tons of metallic zinc. The whole product of the

United States is, of oxide, 10,000 tons, and of spelter, 2,300 tons.

FRANKLINITE is a mineral composed of oxides of iron, zinc and manganese. It is of an iron black color, metallic lustre, and about as hard as feldspar. It is slightly magnetic, and might easily be mistaken for magnetic iron ore.

SUSSEX COUNTY DIRECTORY.

ANDOVER TOWNSHIP.

Abers, Harvey, Andover
Ackerman, Davis, do
Ackerman, John, Newton
Ackerson, Peter, Andover
Ackerson, Jos. do
Ackerson, J. do
Allen, Silas C. do
Anderson, David, do
Ayres, John, Newton
Ayres, Watson, Andover
Babcock, John, Newton
Barber, John do
Barber, Eli W. do
Barber, Wm. do
Barber, Joseph do
Beaty, John, Andover
Beaty, Geo. do
Bennett, Wm. H., do
Bennett, Jas. C. do
Bird, Aaron do
Bird, Peter do
Bird, Thos. do
Blakesley, Wm. E., do
Bouker, Henry, do
Bradford, B. Newton
Busby, ,Alex., Andover
Byram, Daniel T., do
Byram, Horace, do
Case, Geo. B., Newton
Case, Peter M. do
Case, Richard, Andover
Campbell, John, do
Chambers, Geo. do
Chambers, Robert, Andover
Clouse, Wm., Newton
Cook, Levi do
Cook, G. C., Andover
Courtright, Wm., do
Coats, Jas. do
Cox, Chas. C., Newton
Coursen, Allen N., do
Coursen, Jacob L. do
Coursen, Joseph, Andover
Coon, Peter do
Coil, Richard do
Cross, John do
Current, George, Newton
Current, Manning, do
Cunterman, Peter do
Cunterman, J. do
Davidson, Robt., Andover
Davidson, C. S. do
Davidson, Calvin do
Devore, John, Newton
Devore, George, do
Devore, Geo., Jr., do
Devore, Daniel S., do
Devore, Milton do
Devore, C. D. do
Devore, Martin do
Dewley, Isaac do
Demerest, Peter do
Demerest, John do
Decker, Wilson, Andover
Decker, Robt. M., do
Decker, Jno. M. do

Durling, Isaac, Andover
Dunlap, Geo. do
Durham, Benj. do
Eeverett, Geo. do
Ferrell, Daniel, Newton
Ferrell, John do
Fields, John R., Andover
Fields, Wm. do
Freemen, H. M. do
Goble, Richard O., do
Goble, Samuel do
Goble, Jacob do
Graham, Andrew, Newton
Grover, Edgar, Andover
Hamilton, Horace do
Hamilton, Jas. do
Hamilton, Fowler do
Hagert, Jos. W., Newton
Haggerty, Jno. M., do
Hart, Daniel, Andover
Hart, Azariah do
Hart, George do
Hart, Henry do
Harden, Jno. do
Harden, Robt. do
Harden, Samuel do
Heter, John, Newton
Hibler, Thos., Andover
Hibler, Joseph, Newton
Hill, Luther do
Hill, Luther, J., Andover
Hinds, Peter do
Hinds, Wm. do
Hough, M. C. do
Hough, Hedges, Newton
Howe, Freeman, Andover
Houck, Alfred do
Hovenden, Jas. do
Howell, Jno. M., do
Howell, Levi, Newton
Howell, Jonah do
Howell, C. M., Andover
Hunt, Elmer, do
Iliff, Wm. M. do
Johnson, C. P. do
Johnson, John, Andover
Johnson, J. S. do
Johnson, Marshall do
Kay, Peter do
Kinney, Wm. do
Kinney, Horatio do
Kinney, Martin do
Kinnicut, Abram do
Kimball, Peter do
Lawrence, Henry do
Lawrence, Ira do
Lawrence, A. do
Lawless, John do
Layton, E. do
Longcor, J. do
Longcor, Abram do
Longcor, J. L. do
Longcor, J. do
Longcor, Jos. do
Longcor, David do
Maines, Jonathan, do
Maines, N. do
Maines, Peter, Newton
Maines, Jno. do
Martin, Thos. do
Merrin, N. P., Andover
Meachun, Enoch do
Mills, John do
Milham, Jas. do
Miller, Peter do
Miller, John do
Miller, Halsey, Newton
Miller, Geo. do
Misner, W. W., Andover
Misner, Wm. do
Misner, Geo. do
McConnell, A. C., do
McDavitt, Geo. do
McDavitt, Wm. do
McDavitt, W., Jr., do
McDavitt, Jas. do
McDavitt, Stephen do
McDavitt, J. do
McKinney, Wm. do
McManum, Jno., Newton

Nester, Thos., Andover
Oliver, I. do
Orsborn, Chas. do
Orsborn, Ewd. do
Pinkney, John, Newton
Pinkney, Wm. do
Pollard, J. W. do
Puder, Albert do
Quackenbush, Jos. do
Read, Amos do
Rose, Wm. do
Rose, George F. do
Roof, Alfred, Newton
Roof, Theo. do
Roland, Thos., Andover
Rosenkranse, J., do
Sanford, Daniel, do
Schooley, Aaron, do
Sergant, Albert do
Sharp, Peter, Newton
Sharp, Wm., Andover
Shay, Thos., do
Shrickgast, Daniel, Newton
Sidman, Samuel M., Andover
Sidner, John do
Slockbower, Thos. do
Slockbower, John do
Slockbower, C. S. do
Slockbower, Robt. do
Slockbower, M. do
Slater, Wm. M., Newton
Slater, Chas., Andover
Slater, Robt., Newton
Smith, J. T., Andover
Smith, Robt., do
Smith, Pernell do
Snyder, Jos. W., Newton
Space, Jas. do
Space, B. do
Space, J., Jr. do
Space, Levi do
Spitzer, A. do
Struble, Isaac do
Struble, Simeon, Andover
Struble, John A. do

Struble, Amos, Andover
Strader, Jacob, Newton
Strader, John do
Strader, Jos. do
Stickles, Abram do
Stickles, Chas. do
Stickles, Stewart do
Stickles, Dan'l H. do
Stickles, Chas., Jr. do
Stiles, Samuel, Andover
Stiles, Janson K. do
Stiles, John do
Stiles, Morris do
Stiff, Adams do
Stiff, Joseph do
Stiff, James do
Stiff, John do
Stiff, Baltus do
Stackhouse, N. A. do
Stackhouse, Wm. do
Stackhouse, Amos do
Stackhouse, Jonah do
Stackhouse, F. A. do
Stackhouse, David do
Trowbridge, Austin do
Trowbridge, Aaron do
Thorp, Dayton do
Thornhill, Samuel do
Totten, Benj. do
Tuttle, Richard do
Valentine, A. do
Valentine, L. do
Valentine, Jos. do
Van Deren, S., Newton
Van Deren, B. do
Vantassil, Chas., Andover
Vantassil, Wm. do
Vantassil, Jacob do
Washer, Joseph W., Newton
Washer, A., Andover
Washer, Geo., Newton
Washer, Boyles, Andover
Washer, Jos. do
Washer, N. do
Washer, Wm. do

Washer, Amos, Andover
Washer, John do
Washer, John, 2d do
Washer, Robert do
Washer, Robt., Jr. do

Webb, Edw'd, Andover
Whymus, Geo., do
Wilson, David do
Wilson, Geo. do
Wilson, A. H. do
Wilkins, Henry do
Wilcox, Frederick, Andover
Wilgus, Samuel, Newton
Young, Silas, Andover
Young, Lewis do
Young, Jas. do
Young, Wm. do
Young, Michael, Newton

BYRAM TOWNSHIP.

Ackerman, J., Stanhope
Ackerson, Peter, do
Applegate, Jesse, do
Atno, Wm. T., do
Atno, Benj. K. do
Atno, Henry, do
Atno, John, do
Atno, Jos., do
Babb, Coleman, Sparta
Barret, Jno. W., Stanhope
Baldwin, Jeptha do
Bell, Chas., do
Best, Geo. E. do
Best, Dan'l. L., do
Best, Geo., do
Bedford, Albert do
Bedett, Jos., Sparta
Bissell, Jos. H., Stanhope
Black, Jonathan, do
Blinks, Jos., do
Boss, Jos., Andover
Bradbury, Jonathan, Stanhope
Budd, S. D., do
Byrom, Job J., Sparta
Byerly, Robt. L., Stanhope
Case, Jos. H., Waterloo
Cavenaugh, John, Stanhope
Canine, David M., Andover
Canine, David T. do
Clark, Abram L., Stanhope
Clark, Benson S., do
Conn, Jos., Andover
Conn, Theo., Andover
Cottrell, C. J., Stanhope
Coonrod, John, do
Crane, J. J. do
Crosson, S. M., do
Davis, Peter, do
Davis, John, do
Davis, Sidney, do
Dell, Chas. S. do
Dell, John, do
Dennis, Robt., do
Dempster, Wm., do
Decker, Joel, Andover
Downes, John, Stanhope
Donald, Owen, Waterloo
Dockerty, Alex., Stanhope
Dockerty, Wm., do
Dockerty, Jas., Waterloo
Drake, Edward, Stanhope
Drake, George do

Dukin, Charles, Stanhope
Ennis, Wm., do
Fichtor, E., do
Fichtor, John, do
Fluke, John, do
French, James, Waterloo
Glover, John, Stanhope
Glover, Rich., do
Goble, Dan'l W., Andover
Goble, Lewis, Sparta
Groff, Wm., Stanhope
Ham, Geo., Andover
Harvey, Patrick, Stanhope
Haggerty, T. F., do
Hartman, Wm do
Hart, S. B., Andover
Hand, Jon. P., Stanhope,
Hazleton, Henry, Andover
Hazleton, Wm. H., do
Heminover, Watson, Stanhope
Heminover, Elmer, do
Heminover, A. do
Heminover, O., Andover
Helderbrant, Sam'l, Stanhope
Helderbrant, David do
Helderbrant, Robert do
Helderbrant, James, do
Henderson, John, do
Hill, John M., do
Homler, Lambert, Andover
Hothaway, Issac, Stanhope
Howard, James S., do
Hull, Alpheus, do
Huyler, Charles, do
Huyler, Jacob, do
Hunt, Wm., Waterloo
Hubert, George C., Stanhope
Hubert, Lewis L., do
Hulmes, Nathan, do
Ingram, John, Stanhope
Jennings, Jno. F., do
Jones, David, do
Kernes, Charles, Waterloo
Knight, John M. Stanhope
Knight, George T., do
Knight, Thomas, Stanhope
King, Augustus G., do
King, Ridgway, do
Kyte, George C., do
Lampson, L., Sparta
Lantz, David H., do
Laurence, John D., Stanhope
Laurence, F. D., do
Laurence, Wm., Sparta
Laurence, A. S., do
Lewis, George, Stanhope
Lewis, John, do
Lee, A. J., Andover
Lee, Jesse, "
Lee, Wm. H., Stanhope
Lloyd, Henry, do
Lawrence, S. O., do
Lynch, Philip, do
Lynch, Peter, do
Mansfield, Silas, do
Maines, Charles, Sparta
Meeker, Elijah, Waterloo,
Minton, Jacob, Stanhope
Mills, Theo, do
Mooney, George A. do
McConnell, D. W., Sparta
McConnell, Jas. W. Stanhope
McConnell, J., do
McDougal, Wm., do
McDougal, Alfred, do
McDeede, Michael, Waterloo
McGlenn, Patrick, Stanhope
McGill, Gabriel do
McGill, J. do
McGaughlin.
McKain, George, Andover
McKain. Wm., do
McKinney, John, do
McKinney, Robert, do
McKale, Henry, Stanhope
McMullin, Daniel, do
McMullin, Samuel do
McMannis, John, do
McMulty, Barney, do
McMickle, Joseph, Sparta

McNulty, M., Stanhope
McPeak, James, "
McPeak, James, Sparta
McWilliams, John, Stanhope
Neldon, C. R., Stanhope
Niper, George, do
Niper, John, do
Niper, Sidney, do
Niper, Wm. do
Oliver, Henry M., do
Oliver, Joseph, do
Oliver. T. J., do
Oliver, T. J., do
Oliver, Wm., do
Osborn, E. B., do
Palmer, G. G., do
Pettit, James, do
Phelps, Theo., Andover,
Pettinger, A., Stanhope,
Pettinger, A. V., do
Pruden, N., do
Pricket, James, Sparta
Pricket, Stephen, do
Pricket, Sidney, do
Raber, Henry, Stanhope
Rhodes, Benj., do
Rose, Benton, do
Rose, W. B. do
Rose, John R., do
Rose, O. E., Andover
Rose, Nathan, Waterloo
Rose, David, do
Robinson, Seth, Stanhope
Robinson, Wm., Andover
Roloson, Matthias, Sparta
Roloson, D. A., do
Roberts, A. H., Stanhope
Roberts, John do
Rosenkrans, L., do
Roberts, John do
Rowland, Abram, do
Riley, Wm., do
Sanders, Joseph, Sparta
Sanford, G. M., Stanhope
Sanford, C., do
Schoonover, D., Andover
Schoonover, George, Stanhope
Shields, Isaac J., do
Shiner, Isaac, do
Shenan, Thomas, do
Shotwell, Robert, Andover
Sharp, Isaac, Stanhope
Sharp, Joseph "
Sickles, Jesse, "
Sickles, Geo., Sparta
Slockbower, George, Stanhope
Slack, Robert, do
Slack, Michael, do
Slack, Samuel, do
Slack, John J., do
Smith, Wm., do
Smith, James W., do
Smith, Charles J. do
Smith, Peter, Waterloo,
Smith, Samuel T., do
Smith, P. D., do
Smith, Seymour, do
Smith, N. A., do
Smith, Amos, Stanhope,
Stiff, Benjamin, do
Stiff, Charles, do
Stackhouse, A., do
Stackhouse, S. W., Waterloo
Stackhouse, Wm. H., Stanhope
Stackhouse, W. H., Jr., "
Stiles, James, Andover
Stevens, B., "
Strickland, Geo., Stanhope
Stone, D. S., do
Sutton, Wm. W., do
Sutton, Wm. do
Sutton, Charles, do
Sutton, James E., do
Sutton, Wm. do
Sutton, L. F., Andover,
Talmadge, Jas., Stanhope
Tharp, Moses do
Thomas, John, Waterloo
Thomas, J., do
Todd, Wm., Stanhope

Todd, Joseph, Stanhope
Todd, George, do
Todd, John do
Townsend, John, Waterloo
Vanarsdale, J. S., Stanhope
Vandyne, F., do
Vangilder, J. C., do
Ward, George, Waterloo
Ward, Wm., Stanhope
Ward, David, Sparta
Ward, John C., Stanhope
Ward, Ephraim, do
Welsh, Stewart, Sparta
White, John, Stanhope
White, Wm. H., Stanhope
White, S. S., do
Wintermute, C. A., do
Wills, A. S., do
Wills, Samuel, do
Winters, Wm. J., Andover
Wilson, George, do
Wilson, John, Stanhope
Woodruff, John, do
Woodruff, M., do
Wolverton, Wm., Waterloo
Wright, Wm., Stanhope
Wright, C., Andover

FRANKFORD TOWNSHIP.

Abers, John, Branchville
Adams, G. S., do
Adams, Henry, do
Adams, Robert, Augusta
Adams, John B., do
Agney, Henry, Branchville
Allen, Morris, do
Armstrong, G. N., Pakakating,
Armstrong, John B., do
Armstrong, Robert V., do
Aurmick J. L., Branchville
Ayres, James, do
Ayres, Harrison, Beemerville
Ayres, Jesse, do
Ayres, Lebon, do
Ayres, M. D. do
Ayres, Sidney, do
Ayres, Z. O., do
Barbier, F., Branchville
Bales, Peter, do
Bunker, Jeremiah do
Bunker, J. J., do
Beemer, Chas. L., do
Beemer, David C., do
Beemer, Sidney C., do
Beemer, John, Jr., do
Beemer, Albert H. do
Beemer, Pat'k. H. Branehville
Beemer, Robert, do
Bedell, Henry J., do
Bedell, James, Wykertown
Bedell, B. D., do
Bedell, Amzi, Augusta
Bedell, Jacob, Wykertown
Bell, Edw'd. M., Branchville
Bell, S. H., do
Berry, Jacob, Papakating
Bevans, Edwin, Branchville
Betson, Thomas, do
Benson, David D., Papakating
Belden, Wm. H., Branchville
Blanchard, Jeptha, Wykertown
Black, Lewis, Branchville
Bowman, Geo. J., do
Bowman, Edward, do
Bowman, O. S., do
Bowman, George, do
Bond, Smith, do
Bond, Henry, do
Bond, James, do
Brush, Alfred, do
Brink, Evi, do
Bray, John, do
Bray, Ludlow, do

Bray, N. K., Branchville
Butler, Asa, do
Butler, John, do
Butler, Alfred, do
Busekist, Wm., do
Burns, Michael, Papakating
Campbell, C. T., Branchville
Campbell, H., do
Campbell, Wm. D., do
Carnell, J. H., do
Cahro, John, do
Canfield, A. S., do
Carpenter, Austin do
Chamberlain, Morris, do
Chamberlain, Marcus do
Cisco, Lewis F., do
Clark, Thomas, do
Clark, Wallace, Beemerville
Clark, Harmon, Branchville
Clark, W. M., do
Clark, James W., do
Clifford, Martin, do
Clifford, John S., do
Clifford, Harmon, do
Condit, Enos P., do
Courtwright, A. J., do
Courtwright, Wm., do
Courtwright, do
Coss, Jacob A., do
Coss, John J., do
Coss, Ira, do
Coss, Wm. C., do
Coss, Benjamin, do
Coss, Isaac H., do
Compton, Henry J., do
Compton, David, do
Compton, Trueman, do
Compton, Thomas, do
Coursen, Henry B., do
Coursen, Sam'l J., Papakating
Coursen, S. Johnson, do
Coursen, Isaac V., do
Coursen, Jacob A., Branchville
Coursen, Shafer, do
Cole, Halstead, do

Cole, Caleb, Branchville
Cosner, B., Wykertown,
Cosner, Robert, do
Collins, George, Branchville
Crawn, Wm., do
Crane, V. B., do
Crane, Theo., Wykertown,
Crane, A. R., do
Crane, Wm. B., Branchville
Crane, Dr. H. N., do
Crane, Nelson, Papakating
Crane, John W., do
Crisman, V. H., Branchville
Craumer, Wm. M., Augusta
Dalrymple, C. A., Branchville
Dalrymple, Daniel, do
Dalrymple, John do
Dalrymple, James, do
Dalrymple, Richard, do
Dalrymple, Squire, do
Dalrymple, Wm. H. do
Decker, A. O., do
Decker, Harrison H., do
Decker, John M., do
Decker, S. R., do
Decker, Richard, Augusta
Decker, Andrew, Papakating
Dekay, John, do
Dennis, Peter, Augusta,
De Witt, Wm. W., do
De Witt, Wm. L., Branchville
Degrote, Amzi, Papakating,
Devenport, Marcus, Branch'lle
Dermond, J. H., do
Divies, James, do
Dilliston, De Alton, Beemer'lle
Dilliston, John, Branchville
Dimon, J. N. V., do
Doland, David, Papakating
Doty, Wesley, Branchville
Drake, Benjamin A., do
Drake, N., do
Durling, Joseph, do
Duuning, Edgar A., do
Everett, Allen, do

Everitt, Joseph G., Branchville
Everitt, John L., do
Everitt, Chas. W., Augusta
Everitt, Samuel A., do
Farris, Samuel, Wykertown
Feezlacr, John, Branchville
Foster, Stephen, do
Foster, H. P., do
Fountain, Henry S., do
Gessner, Edward, do
Gessner, Henry, do
Gould, Jacob C., Papakating
Gould, Elias, do
Gordon, C. R., Branchville
Gregory, Lewis, do
Groover, G. J., Augusta
Gray, Wm., Branchville
Haines, J. Allen, do
Haines, Tobias do
Hannah, James, do
Handy, Abram, do
Haggerty, James, do
Haggerty, B., do
Hazen, Allen C., do
Hancey, John G., do
Hetzel, J. S., do
Hedges, Dr. Jos., do
Hewitt, Richard, do
Hinkle, S. H., do
Hockenberg, P. G., Papakating
Horton, George, Branchville
Holden, W. J., do
Holden, Nicholas, do
Hopkins, Abram C., do
Hooey, Elisha, do
Hollon, Isaac, do
Holton, Wm. H., do
Hough, John, do
Hough, Alex., do
Hough, Wm., do
Hough, S. H., Wykertown
Holly, Timothy, Branchville
Howell, Janson P., do
Howell, Wm. H., Wykertown
Hunt, John C., Branchville
Hunt, Stephen, Branchville
Hunt, Andrew C., do
Hull, Porter, do
Ike, Albert, do
Ike, George, do
Ike, I aac, do
Jarvis, James M., do
Johnson, P., do
Johnson, Theodore, do
Johnson, Wm. W., do
Johnson, J. A., Wykertown
Johnson, Thomas, do
Kaiser, John, Branchville
Keen, William, do
Keepers, John M., Augusta
Kimball, Daniel, Branchville
Kimball, George, do
Kymer, C. E., Wykertown
Kymer, F. B., Branchville
Kymer, James C. do
Kymer, John do
Kymer, David L. do
Kymer, B. P. do
Lantz, George, Augusta
Lantz, M. F. do
Lantz, John, Branchville
Lantz, George, Jr., Branchville
Litz, Halsey, Papakating
Langcor, Jacob, Branchville
Lundy, Wm. C. do
Lindsley, Silas do
Mattison, Wm. do
Martin, Elijah, Augusta
Martin, Lewis, do
Malone, Charles, Papakating
Malone, Charles, Jr., do
Marvin, Daniel, Branchville
Mathis, John B. do
Meddaugh, Wm. do
Mills, Peter, Augusta
Morris, Peter, Branchville
Morris, Peter J. do
Morris, Jacob N. do
Morris, Isaac do
Morris, John do

Morris, Jacob, Branchville
Morris, D. J. do
Moore, William do
Myres, Nelson, Papakating
McCoy, James, Branchville
McCarrick, James do
McDanolds, W. W. do
McDanolds, J. M. do
McDanolds, Joseph do
McDanolds, John S. do
McDanolds, Wm. do
McDanolds, Cris., Papakating
McKee, Hugh, Branchville
McKee, John do
McMickel, Robert, Augusta
McMillen, Thos., Branchville
McNara, Daniel do
Nixon, Allen do
Nixon, Silas do
Norcross, Jacob do
Northrup, James do
O'Brien, James do
Osborne, Jos. A., Papakating
Perigo, John, Branchville
Perigo, Thomas do
Perigo, Thomas, Jr. do
Peters, A. L. do
Pellet, S. J., Papakating
Pellet, R. W. do
Pettit, John, Branchville
Pettit, Samuel do
Phillips, Lynch do
Phillips, Chas. L. do
Phillips, Henry, do
Phillips, Nelson, Papakating
Phillips, Nelson B., Branch'lle
Phillips, Henry, Jr. do
Phillips, Jesse C. do
Phillips, Allen do
Phillips, Simon do
Phillips, Jesse H. do
Phillips, George do
Pitney, George, Augusta
Plumstead, E., Branchville
Price, Samuel B. do

Price, Z. H., Papakating
Price, Jos. W., Branchville
Predmore, D. H., do
Predmore, Insley do
Preston, John, do
Rancher, Lewis do
Riker, Jerome do
Riker, Wm. B. do
Riker, Theodore do
Roe, Nathaniel do
Roe, N. S. do
Roe, Lewis do
Roe, Chas., Jr. do
Roe, James do
Roe, John do
Roe, John H. do
Roe, Wm. C. do
Roe, Edward, do
Roe, Wm. H. do
Roe, Jesse G. do
Roe, Jacob do
Roe, Leonard, Augusta
Roleson, H. J., Branchville
Roberts, James do
Rorabach, Jno H. do
Rodimer, David do
Rodimer, A. H., do
Rodimer, Theo. do
Rodimer, Peter do
Ross, Jacob, Augusta
Rodney, Morris, Branchville
Rosenkrans, Theo. do
Rutan, Wm. H. do
Rutan, Hudson, Papakating
Rutan, Peter D., Branchville
Rutan, D. H., do
Rutan, Dan'l H. do
Rutan, Adam C. do
Ryerson, Wm., do
Sanders, Warren, do
Savere, John W. do
Schooley, George, do
Shotwell, J. J. do
Shay, Hiram do
Shay, C. B. do

Shay, E. Branchville
Shay, James M. do
Shay, Wesley, Augusta
Sherred, John, Branchville
Silcox, James, do
Simmons, Z. do
Silsbee, David do
Smith, Samuel P., Wykertown
Smith; James P. do
Smith, H. Augusta
Smith, H. J., Branchville
Smith, N. C. do
Smith, Samuel do
Snook, Jonas do
Snook, Peter do
Snook, Robert do
Snook, A. J. do
Snook, Coleman do
Snook, Philip do
Snook, Chas. S. do
Snook, Jos. do
Snook, Henry do
Snable, Abram do
Spanganburg, M. S. do
Spanganburg, Chas. do
Spanganburg, Philip do
Spanganburg, Jesse do
Spanganburg, T. M. do
Spanganburg, Alma do
Spargo, James do
Spargo, Abram do
Spargo, Benjamin do
Spicher, S. do
Struble, Richard do
Struble, David do
Struble, Jacob do
Struble, J. A. O. do
Struble, James H. do
Struble, Wm. do
Struble, John do
Struble, Jas. J., Augusta
Struble, Canfield do
Stephens, Elisha, Branchville
Stephenfield, Jas. do
Stephenfield, Theo. Branchv'le
Stephenfield, John, do
Stoll, Jos. A. do
Stoll, Abram do
Stoll, Jacob do
Strader, Wm. H., Wykertown
Strader, Jos. D., Augusta
Strader, Jos. H. do
Sullivan, Chas. T., Branchville
Teel, A. B. do
Thompson, John do
Tooker, Samuel do
Truesdell, Jas. do
Truax, G. do
Trainer, T. D. do
Troger, Laurence do
Utter, John J. do
Utter, H. S. do
Vanduzer, Geo. A., Branchville
Vannetten, Daniel do
Vanauken, J. S. do
Vanauken, W. J. do
Vanauken, A. C., Wykertown
Vanauken, B. do
Valentine, C. W., Papakating
Washer, Jas., Branchville
Walton, John do
Westbrook, J. C. do
Westbrook, R. S. do
Whitaker, Henry do
Winters, Isaac do
Williams, A. L. do
Williams, S. H. do
Williams, Isaac D. do
Williams, Albert do
Williams, John do
Williamson, Jas. H. do
Wickham, G. J. do
Winters, L., Augusta
Wyker, Daniel, Branchville
Wyker, Lynch D. do
Wyker, Philip do
Wyker, Halsey do

GREEN TOWNSHIP.

Ackerson, M. A., Tranquility
Armstrong, Geo., do
Armstrong, Wm., do
Armstrong, J. L., do
Auble, Jos. N., Andover
Auble, George, Hunts Mills
Ayres, John H., Tranquility
Ayres, Jos., Huntsville
Ayres, A do
Berry, Watson T., Hunts Mills
Berry, Samuel, Lincoln
Bennett, Isaiah, do
Bennett, A. S. do
Bell, Elias, Tranquility
Bird, George C., Andover
Boroman, J., Tranquility
Booth, Andrew, Hunts Mills
Briskey, John, Lincoln
Case, A. S. do
Calvin, L. B. Hunts Mills
Calvin, L. W., do
Chambers, Wm., do
Chandler, Wm., Huntsville
Coil, Geo. P., Lincoln
Cook, Elisha, Andover
Collins, J. W. Tranquility
Coats, S. W., do
Cooper, C. C. do
Coleman, John do
Cramer, Geo. S., Lincoln
Crispin, Silas, Tranquility
Crispin, Benj., Huntsville
Currant, George, Hunts Mills
Decker, J. J., Tranquility.
Dence, Wm., Huntsville
Dence, Japtha, do
Dennis, Wm. R., Lincoln
Dennis, Jacob, do
Dobbins, Pat'k, Andover
Dormada, Henry, Tranquility
Dildine, Ralph, Hunts Mills
Dildine, Henry, do
Drake, Geo. B., do
Drake, V. S., Huntsville
Drake, J. C., Lincoln
Drake, E. P., do
Drake, J. M., do
Drake, S. H., do
Drake, Jacob B., Tranquility
Drake, Hezekiah do
Dunn, Joseph, do
Dunn, Alex., do
Emmons, David, Hunts Mills,
Emmons, A. S., do
Farley, Wm., do
Fox, J., do
Folkner, Jas. M., Lincoln
Freeman, Jas. H., do
Fredericks, Nelson, Andover
Gillam Thos. D., Lincoln
Greer, John, Hunts Mills
Greer, Geo., do
Grey, Jno., do
Grey, Wm. C., do
Groover, John, do
Hand, Chas., do
Hardick, Nelson do
Hardin, Robert, do
Hardin, Philip, do
Hardin, Sylvester, Tranquility
Hays, Thos., do
Hamler, Abner, do
Hamler, David, do
Hamler, N. B., Huntsville
Hart, Wm. H., do
Hart, Jno. W., Huntsville
Hawk, Jno. S., Lincoln
Hamilton, Wm., Tranquility
Hedden, Thos., Lincoln
Heater, J. V., Hunts Mills
Hibler, M. S., Lincoln
Hibler, W. H., do
Hibler, J. A., Tranquility
Hill, Sam'l, Andover
Howell, Dan'l W., Hunts Mills
Hunt, Jos. B., do

Hunt, T. F., Hunts Mills
Hunt, Sam'l H., Lincoln
Hull, Cornelius do
Huffman, Henry, Huntsville
Hubert, Jos., Tranquility
Kenady, Jno. L., do
Kenady, E. V., do
Keepers, A. C., Lincoln
Kyle, Wm., Hunts Mills
Lanning, Geo., Huntsville
Lambert, J. C., Lincoln
Lawrence, Syl., Tranquility
Labar, Jno. S., do
Labar, Frank, Lincoln
Labar, Wm., do
Lewis, Silas, Tranquility
Lougeor, Anthony, Lincoln
Lougcor, Alonzo, do
Lougcor, John, do
Lougcor, Theo., do
Maines, Jessie T., Tranquility
Miller, Henry N., Hunts Mills
Miller, Robt. R., do
Ming, N. R., do
Morrison, Wm., do
McCormick, Edw., do
Nicholas, Lewis J. do
Nugent, John do
Oakes, Andrew, Huntsville
Orner, Guy, Andover
Patterson, W. H., Tranquility
Philips, Barret, Huntsville
Philips, John, do
Pierson, Jos., Hunt Mills
Porter, Geo. W. do
Porter, Dan'l A. do
Quackenbush, J. S., Huntsville
Quick, Michael, Hunts Mills
Read, Luthur H., Tranquility
Read, Nathaniel, do
Reaves, Jas., Hunts Mills
Roy, Wm. C., do
Roy, Dan'l H., do
Roe, Jacob do
Roe, George, do
Roe, John, Hunts Mills
Roe, Dan'l C. do
Roe, Albert, Tranquility
Roe, Hudson, Lincoln
Rose, Benj. M., Hunts Mills
Runion, Watson, Tranquility
Runion, A. B., do
Runion, Wm. T., Huntsville
Runion, H. V., do
Shaw, Geo., do
Sharp, Peter do
Sharp, Wm. H. do
Sharp, Jos. A., Tranquility
Shaver, Casper, Lincoln
Shaver, A. E., do
Shawyer, Geo. W., Tranquility
Singular, Anthony, Lincoln
Stockbower, M. R., do
Sliker, Bradford, Hunts Mills
Smith, Levi M., Tranquility
Snook, Isaac C., Hunts Mills
Snook, Wm., do
Snook, Alfred, do
Steele, Robt., Huntsville.
Steele, Moses do
Straley, Isaac A. do
Stiles, John, Lincoln
Stinson, J. B., do
Stall, J. do
Stang, Henry, do
Stackhouse, J. P., Lincoln
Stackhouse, Chas., do
Stackhouse, L. M., Huntsville
Stafford, J. R., Hunts Mills
Sutton, Chas., Huntsville
Sutton, Andrew, do
Taylor, Geo., Tranquility
Teats, Jonathan, Hunts Mills
Tillman, Edw., do
Van Syckle, R., Huntsville
Van Syckle, Wm., do
Van Syckle, Jas., do
Van Syckle, Sam'l, do
Van Syckle, W. S., do
Van Syckle, Jas. J., Lincoln

Vass, A. F., Lincoln
Vass, Clinton, Tranquility
Vought, A. J., do
Vought, J. L., do
Vought, J. T., Lincoln
Vreeland, J. H., Tranquility
Vreeland, Jacob, do
Warbáss, D. R., Hunts Mills
Walker, John, do
White, Nicholas, Lincoln
Wilson, Lewis, Huntsville
Wilson, Sam'l H., Huntsville
Wilson, Obed O., do
Wilson, John, Hunts Mills
Wilcox, P. M., do
Windel, Timothy, Tranquility
Wintermute, L., do
Wintermute, A. S., Lincoln
Wilgus, W. G., Huntsville
Wolfe, Theo., Tranquility
Wolfe, Wm., do
Wolfe, John, Lincoln
Wolover, Jno. W., Hunts Mills
Young, Theo., Huntsville
Young, Saml'l W., do

HAMPTON TOWNSHIP.

Ackerson, M., Pleasant Valley
Anderson, Samuel, Newton
Anderson, Benjamin do
Anderson, John do
Anderson, Benj., Jr. do
Anderson, Benj. A. do
Anderson, Thos. G. do
Authany, Peter, do
Bale, John, Pleasant Valley
Bale, A. J. do
Bale, A. O. do
Barber, Samuel do
Barker, William, Newton
Babcock, John do
Beach, Benj. do
Beatty, James do
Bray, John do
Cassidy, Geo. do
Cassidy, Samuel do
Cassidy, Samuel 2d. do
Case, B. S. do
Case, Elmer do
Case, Peter do
Campbell, Daniel do
Couse, E. A. do
Couse, David do
Couse, John do
Couse, W. H. Newton
Coursen, Geo. H. do
Coursen, Jno. S. do
Coursen, Winfield do
Cox, Austin do
Cox, Wm. M. do
Cox, Dalas do
Couclin, Geo. do
Couclin, R. N. do
Couclin, Jas. do
Compton, Lewis, Branchville
Crawn, Jacob S., Newton
Crawn, A. R. do
Crawn, Jas. do
Crawn, Simon do
Crawn, Wm. do
Crawn, W. S., Swartswood
Curry, E. M., Pleasant Valley
Curry, B. B. do
Dennis, Nathan, Newton
Decker, Jas. do
Decker, Thos. do
Decker, Joseph do
Doel, Chas. do
Doel, Theo. do
Doty, David do
Drake, Wm. do

Emery, John Newton
Freeman, A. H. do
Fitts, Jas. G. do
Garris, Samuel do
Griggs, Aaron do
Griggs, Henry J. do
Grage, John do
Grover, Joseph do
Grover, Elijah do
Grover, Geo. do
Grover, Martin, Swartswood
Grover, Horace, Pl'sant Valley
Hawk, G. F., Newton
Hawk, Edward, do
Hawk, Jno. W. do
Hague, Benj. do
Hardin, Jas. do
Hardin, Wm. S. do
Harhaus, Theo. do
Harding, Theo. do
Hankerson, J. R. do
Hankerson, S. G. do
Hankerson, S. W. do
Hankerson, Lewis do
Harty, Jas. do
Hendershot, Israel do
Hendershot, A. do
Hendershot, Peter, do
Hendershot, T. J. do
Hendershot, Geo. do
Hendershot, J. A. do
Hendershot, Jno., Swartswood
Hendershot, P. L., Pl'nt Valley
Hendershot, Wm. do
Hedden, David, Swartswood
Hill, Adam W., Newton
Horton, Geo. do
Holmes, C. do
Huston, Chas. do
Huston, Aaron do
Huston, G. do
Johnson, Jno. D. do
Johnson, Peter do
Jones, Jno. G. do
Kein, Jno., Swartswood

Kint, Jos. Swartswood
Kint, Jos. Jr. do
Kint, Isaac do
Kint, Jas. do
Kitchcart, Dan'l do
Kitchcart, D. W. do
Lane, Barnes, Newton
Lewis, Samuel do
Marsh, Stephen do
Maines, C. S., Pleasant Valley
Maines, Elias, Newton
Maines, Wm. do
Meeker, Aaron do
Meeker, Jno. H. do
Merring, Amzi do
Merring, Elias do
Merring, A. Pleasant Valley
Merring, Isaac, Newton
Moore, Wm. do
Moore, David do
Morris, Abram S. do
Morris, Wm. R. do
Morris, Benj. C. do
Morris, Wm., Pleasant Valley
Morris, Elias do
Morris, Oliver do
Morris, A. M. do
Morris, Alpheus, Swartswood
McCan, Richard, Newton
McPeek, I. B. do
Northrup, R. V. do
Northrup, F. B. do
Northrup, H. C. do
Northrup, M. W. do
Northrup, P. T., Pl'ant Valley
Ogden, Robert, Newton
Oliver, Oscar do
Oliver, Jas. L. do
Oliver, A. S. do
Ousted, Abraham do
Ousted, Jno. J. do
Paugh, Geo. do
Pettit, Geo. M. do
Pittinger, Thos. do
Pittinger, Abram, Swartswood

Pittinger, Wm. Swartswood
Predmore, Wm., Newton
Predmore, Jno. M. do
Roof, Christopher do
Roof, Jno. N. do
Roof, P. M. do
Roof, S. H. do
Robbins, Jno., Pleasant Valley
Robbins, Patrick do
Rutan, Jno. do
Ryerson, Geo. M., Newton
Ryerson, Thos. C. do
Savercool, Wm., Pl'ant Valley
Searls, Geo. R. do
Shotwell, Wm. J., Newton
Shotwell, Geo. A. do
Shotwell, J. E. do
Sheler, Robert do
Shupe, David do
Shay, Jas. do
Sherred, R., Pleasant Valley
Sherred, Jacob do
Snider, Joseph, Newton
Snider, Peter do
Snook, Jno., Pleasant Valley
Snook, Wm. do
Snook, Hiram do
Snook, Henry do
Snook, Elias, Newton
Smith, Jas. P. do
Smith, Peter do
Smith, A. O. do
Smith, C. H. do
Smith, J. B. do
Smith, P. A. do
Smith, Chas. H., do
South, H. do
South, Jas. do
South, G. do
South, Jacob, do
Space, Wm., Pleasant Valley
Space, Henry, Newton
Stickles, Z. B. do
Stoll, Ephraim Newton
Stoll, Albert do
Struble, D. H. Pleasant Valley
Struble, Oliver do
Struble, Philip L. do
Struble, Thos. do
Struble, Wm. P. do
Struble, P. W. do
Struble, Nelson do
Struble, Leonard do
Struble, Jno. A. do
Struble, O. B. do
Struble, Leonard, Jr. do
Struble, Jno. D. do
Struble, Albert do
Struble, Jno. J. do
Struble, Thos. P. do
Struble, Wallace do
Struble, George, Newton
Strader, Moses N. do
Swartswelder, Jno. do
Thompson, Hiram do
Titsworth, Martin do
Totten, W. P. do
Truax, Gabriel, do
Van Fleet, Alfred do
Van Horne, Henry do
Van Sickle, C. B. do
Vanatte, Jno., Pleasant Valley
Vanatte, H. do
Vandoren, H. H., Newton
Wallen, Isaiah, do
Ward, Frank M. do
Westbrook, Jno. W. do
Westbrook, Jno. A. do
Wilcox, Johnson do
Wilcox, Aaron do
Winters, Alf'd, Pleasant Valley
Williams, M., do
Williams, Samuel, Newton
Williams, Chas. M., do
Williams, Andrew do

HARDYSTON TOWNSHIP.

Ackerson, Nich., Monroe Cor.
Agany, James, Franklyn
Agany, Michael. do
Allen, Barney, do
Allen, Thomas, do
Allington, John do
Anderson, George, Hamburg
Babcock, M., Franklin
Babcock, Ira do
Babcock, Peter P., Stockholm
Babcock, Sam'l do
Ball, George, Hamburg
Beardslee, Jonas, Ogdensburg
Beardslee, David S., do
Beardslee, Elias, Franklin
Beardslee, Sam'l A. Hamburg
Beardslee, Theo. R., do
Beaty, Jas., Stockholm
Beaumont, George, Ogdensb'g
Belcher, John, Hamburg
Belcher, Peter, Franklin
Belcher, John A., Hamburg
Bellew, Jacob, do
Bellew, Mark, do
Benjamin, N. E. do
Berrigan, William, Franklin
Bishop, Benjamin, Hamburg
Bishop, John, Franklin
Black, John A., do
Brink, George, do
Brink, Adams, do
Bross, William, Hamburg
Bross, G. L., do
Brown, Joseph, Stockholm
Brown, States, Franklin
Brown, John C., do
Brown, William, Stockholm
Brown, John L., Franklin
Bunn, Obediah, Hamburg
Burrows, Joseph, do
Butler, Jas., Franklin
Card, Samuel F., Stockholm
Carman, Peter C. do
Carpenter Alex., Hamburg.
Carrigan, Owen, Franklin
Case, James G., do
Case, John O., do
Case, Winfield S. do
Case, Edward A., do
Cassady, Edward, Hamburg.
Cassady, Abram, do
Cassady, Michael, Franklin
Cassady, Daniel, Hamburg
Caton, Richard, Stockholm
Caton, Wm. P., Hamburg
Chambers, Sam'l, Ogdensburg
Chambsrlain, Mahl., Ogdensb'g
Chardavine H., Beaver Run
Cisco Giles, Hamburg
Cisco, Giles, jr., do
Clark, John W., Franklin
Coan, Daniel, do
Coan, John, do
Coan, Michael, do
Coats, William, do
Coddington, John, Hamburg
Coe, Edward, Franklin
Coleman, John, do
Congleton, J. E., Beavers Run
Conklin, John, Franklin
Conner Hiram, Hamburg
Connar, Lemuel, do
Connally, Michel, Franklin
Couplin, James H., Hamburg
Couse, Dr. J. P., Franklin
Cox, John, Hamburg
Cox, Nicholas J., Hamburg
Crabtree, James, Stockholm
Crawley, Timothy, Franklin
Crawley, Jerry, do
Cronan, William do
Cuddy, John do
Cumming, Peter, do
Curran, William, Ogdensburg
Davenport, Lewis, Hamburg
Davenport, L. D., Stockholm

Davenport, John, Stockholm
Davis, Horace L., Franklin
Day, Silas, do
Day, David, do
Day, Clark, Hamburg
Day, Clark M., Stockholm
Day, Ezra H., do
Decker, Theodore, Hamburg
Degraw, Henry, Stockholm
Denike, James, Franklin
Dennis, Jesse do
Dennis, J. Wesley, Beaver Run
Desmou, Michal, Franklin
Dewitt, James, Hamburg
Dolan, William, Franklin
Dolan, Wm., Jr., Franklin
Dolan, Daniel J., Beaver Run
Dimston, John, Franklin
Dorman, John do
Doremus, Richard, Stockton
Drake, Jacob, do
Dunn, William do
Dunn, James, do
Dunn, Edwin do
Dunn, Wm. H., do
Durling, Sidney, Franklin
Edsall, Henry W., Hamburg
Edsall, Joseph, Franklin
Edsall, Wm. H. Hamburg
Edsall, Benj. H., do
Edsall, Richard, do
Edsall, Thos. J., do
Edsall, R. E., do
Edwards, William, Franklin
Elson, E. M., Hamburg
Ervin Martin, Stockholm
Everman, Joseph, Franklin
Evermore, George, do
Fitzgibbons, David, do
Fitzgerald, David, do
Flood, Mathias, do
Flood, Edward do
Flinn, Gilbert, do
Foha, John do
Foha, Patrick, do
Force, John, Hamburg
Fountain, Arch., do
Fountain, Peter, do
Eountain, Thos., do
Fowler, Henry O., Franklin
Fredericks, Wm., do
Frederick, Jas. J., Stockholm
Frost, James, Franklin
Garrison, Isaac, do
Gilson, Hugh, Hamburg
Goble, Zophar, Ogdensburg
Graham, James, Franklin
Green, Martin, Hamburg
Green, Albert, Franklin
Green, Charles, do
Greer, George W., Stockholm
Grimes, John, Franklin
Grimes, Patrick, do
Grimes, Thomas, do
Grogan, Martin, do
Haines, Hon. Dan'l, Hamburg
Haines, Rev. A. A., do
Hamilton, Fowler, do
Hamilton, James M., do
Hamiltoo, John B., do
Harden, H. J., Beaver Run
Harden, J. V., do
Havens, Horace, do
Henderson, John, Stockholm
Henderson, M., do
Hendershot, J. B., Hamburg
Hendrew, Richard, Franklin
Hickey, Daniel, do
Hiles, William, Beaver Run
Hiles, J. S., do
Holden, A. M., do
Holley, Edward, Franklin
Holley, Michael, Stockholm
Hopkins, A., Monroe Corner.
Howell, Timothy, Franklin
Inglish, James R., Monroe Cor.
Johnson, Elijah, Franklin
Jones, John V., Beaver Run
Jones, B. K., do
Jones, Daniel, do

Kelley, Patrick, Franklin
Kimball, John W., Stockholm
Kimball, John N., do
Kimball, Wm., J. S., Franklin
Kimball, M. R., Hamburg
Kimball, Garret, Franklin
Kimball, E. M., Monroe Cor.
Kimball, Daniel, do
Kimball, Rob't F., Franklin
Kimball, Geo. W., Stockholm
Kincade, Edward, do
King, John, Franklin
Lacey, James, do
Lacey, John, do
Lang, Robert, do
Lantz, Wm. M., Monroe Cor.
Lantz, Jacob, Franklin
Lantz, John P., do
Larow, Elton, do
Laughlin, Thos., do
Lawrence, L. M., Hamburg
Lawrence, Thos., do
Lawrence, Hugh T., Franklin
Lemine, William, do
Lennice, Thomas, do
Lennice, Thomas, Jr., do
Lewis Daniel D., Stockholm
Lewis, Wm. S., Franklin
Lewis, James M., Stockholm
Linn, W. , Dr., Hamburg
Linn, D. R., do
Longstreet, Wm. S., Franklin
Loftus, Anthony, Franklin
Losey, Samuel R., do
Lozaw, William, Hamburg
Loftus, Ira, Stockholm
Mains, Wm., Monroe Corners
Magee, Benjamin, Stockholm
Margerum, Noah H., do
Margerum David E., do
Martin, Nathan, Hamburg
Masachar, William, Stockholm
Masachar, John do
Masachar, John, Jr., do
Masachar, John M., do
Masachar, John A., Stockholm
Masachar, Jacob, do
McGovern, Hugh, Franklin
McManus, Charles, Hamburg
McCann, Joel, do
McCann, John, do
McCann, Jacob, do
McPeak, James, Monroe Cor.
McPeak, George, do
Miller, Edward, Franklin
Mitten, Daniel B., Hamburg
Mitten, William do
Minion, J. M., Monroe Cor.
Morgan, C. W., Franklin
Morgan, Robert, do
Morrison, Edward, Franklin
Montonye, James, do
Monell, Charles L., Hamburg
Monell, John B., do
Mulligan, Thomas, Franklin
Mulvey, James, do
Munson, Edward, do
Murphy, John, do
Nichols, John W., Stockholm
Oats, William, Franklin
O'Daniols, Michael, Franklin
O'Daniels, John, do
O'Daniels, Martin, do
O'Daniels, Patrick, do
O'Maley, Miles, do
Osborne, Richard, Hamburg
Parker, William do
Peacock, William, Stockholm
Pellet, LeG. W., Hamburg
Pellet, Dr. J. B., do
Pelloubet, Isaac, do
Pelloubet, Estall, do
Pettinger, Samuel, Stockholm
Pierson, Wm. J. do
Pierson, William do
Pierson, Charles do
Pollison, Israel, do
Pollison, Wm. H., Jr. do
Pollison, Theodore, do
Pollison, John A., do

Pollison, Selah, Stockholm
Pollison, Wm. H., do
Potter, L., Beaver Run
Potter, E. M., Monroe Cor.
Potter, Elias, do
Price, S. O., Franklin
Quigby, Thos. do
Quinn, Patrick, do
Rice, Edward, Monroe Cor.
Richard, Jos., Franklin
Rigg, N. C., Stockholm
Rigg, T. D., Hamburg
Robinson, Sam'l, Franklin
Robinson, Sam'l, Jr., do
Robinson, John, Hamburg
Roaddy, William, Franklin
Rooney, Thomas, do
Ross, George M., Stockholm
Ross, Thomas, J., do
Ross, Thomas, do
Rude, Robert, W., Hamburg
Rude, Joseph, do
Rude, A. F., do
Rude, John P. do
Rude, Thos. J., do
Rude, Wm. B., do
Rude, Sam'l P., do
Rude, Issachar, Stockholm
Rude, William, Hamburg
Rude, Wm. H., do
Rude, Horace E. do
Rude, George W., do
Rude, Barton E. do
Rude, George J., Stockholm
Scott, Charles W., Franklin
Scott, Stephen, do
Scott, James G., do
Scott, Caleb H., Hamburg
Shauger, Jacob, Ogdensburg
Sheldon, Sam'l, Monroe Cor.
Shepard, Mathias, Franklin
Shepard, Jacob, do
Shepard, Jacob, Jr., do
Shepard, G. M., Stockholm
Silver, Rev. David, Hamburg
Simpson, John F., Franklin
Simpson, Abram L. do
Simpson, Frank H. do
Simpson, Henry I., Hamburg
Simpson, William, do
Simpson, Horace, do
Simpson, Alanson, do
Simpson, Silah, Franklin
Simpson, Peter, do
Simpson, Thomas, do
Siater, J. J. B., Monroe Cor.
Smith, Peter, Hamburg
Smith, Thos., do
Smith, Steward do
Smith, Frekerick, do
Smith, Stephen, Hamburg
Smith, Stephen, Jr., do
Smith, William, do
Smith, John J., Franklin
Smith, Elias, do
Smith, Jacob, do
Smith, J. C., do
Smith, Charles, do
Smith, Samuel, do
Smith, Frank, do
Smith, George, do
Smith, Barney, do
Smith, Wm. S., Hamburg
Stickles, S. H., Stockholm
Stoll, Lewis, Franklin
Stoll, Sidney, do
Strait, Hiram, Stockholm
Strait, D., do
Strait, William, Stockholm
Strait, Abram, do
Strait, Amzi, do
Strait, John S. do
Struble, Hugh, Hamburg
Struble, Philip, Monroe Cor.
Talmage, Jacob M., Franklin
Tidaback, Wm., Ogdensburg
Tidaback, Dan'l., Monroe Cor.
Tidaback, David, Franklin
Tidaback, Jacob, do
Tinkey, D. W., Hamburg

Dennis, Evi, Lafayette
Demarest, John P. do
Demarest, John T. do
Demarest, Elias P. do
Demarest, John do
Dennis, James do
Titus Daniel, Beaver Run
Titus, George, Franklin
Totted, John, Ogdensburg
Trusdall, Jesse, Stockholm
Valentine, Benj. R., Hamburg
Vandroof, Wm., Franklin
Vanorden, James, Hamburg
Vanorden, Ira, do
Vanstrander, P., do
Yetman, Wm., do
Young, John W., Beaver Run
Wade, N., Ogdensburg,
Wade, Winfield, Franklin
Walter, Charles, Stockholm
Walters, George do
Wayner, Cris., Franklin

Webb, William, Franklin
Webb, Abner, Stockholm
Werden, James, Hamburg
Welch, Thomas, Hamburg
Welh, Jos., Hamburg
Welch, Martin, Franklin
Willis, William, do
Willis, Aaron, do
Willis, Joe, do
Williams, Alonzo J., Hamburg
Williams, J. W., do
Williams, A. R., do
Williams, Benj., Stockholm
Wilson, Samuel, Hamburg
Wilson, John P., do
Winters, Henry, Franklin
Winans, George W., Stockholm
Woods, William B., Hamburg
Weods, Jonas S., do
Woods, James, Stockholm
Wood, Israel, Franklin
Wood, George T.F ,ranklin

LAFAYETTE TOWNSHIP.

Ackerson, Peter, Lafayette
Ackerson, Jno. D. do
Ackerson, Nelson, do
Ackerson, Wm. N. do
Ackerson, C. D. do
Ackerson, Ralph do
Ackerson, Jas. M. do
Ackerson, Gilbert do
Ackerson, Ford, do
Ackerson, Emanuel, do
Ackerson, A. R. do
Adams, Jno. D. do
Allen, Jno. L. do
Anderson, Wm., do
Anderson, A. J. do
Armstrong, O. P. do
Armstrong, Wm. L., do
Ayres, Benj. do
Backster, Geo., do
Backster, John J. do
Barkman, Chas. do
Beagle, A. H. do

Bell, John, Lafayette
Blanchard, Samuel, do
Brodt, Levi do
Butler, Jos. do
Buntiug, Wm. A. do
Case, Jas. P. do
Case, Wm. S. do
Case, Walter R. do
Carpenter, Jacob do
Cahow, Daniel do
Chandler, Wm. do
Chew, Chas. do
Clark, Geo. do
Collver, Geo. W. do
Collver, David J. do
Collver, Nathan do
Collver, G. do
Courtright, Dan'l C., do
Cope, A. P., do
Cox, Joseph do
Current, Joseph do
Demarest, C. D. do

Dennis, Chas. H. Lafayette
Dobbs, Wm. do
Dorinda, Thos. do
Dorinda, Benj. S. do
Dodd, John F. do
Drake, Geo. do
Durling, A. J. do
Dusenbery, J. A. Beaver Run
Emmons, Wm., Lafayette
Emons, Jacob, do
Emons, Albert, do
Everett, James do
Fastic, Samuel do
Fisk, Thomas L. do
Fletcher, R. G. do
Fletcher, D. do
Gray, Wm. do
Griffith, Chas. do
Grover, Wm. do
Gunderman, J. C. do
Gunderman, Samuel, do
Hagaman, J. B. do
Hagaman, J. W. do
Hance, Henry do
Havens, Robert do
Hiles, Wm. do
Hiles, Thos. J. do
Howell, Wm. do
Howell, Wm., Jr., do
Howell, Thos. do
Hogan, John do
Hough, Peter do
Hopper, Daniel do
Hopkins, Benj. do
Hopkins, Jno. do
Hopkins, Phillip do
Hopkins, Alfred do
Hopkins, Benj., Jr., do
Hoppaugh, Wm. do
Hoffman, Geo. do
Huston, Jas. B. do
Huston, Mark do
Hull, John M. do
Hunting, Wm. do
Hurd, L. B., do
Humphry, Richard Lafayette
Ingersoll, Gilbert do
Ingersoll, Samuel do
Johnson, Jos. do
Jones, Jas. N. do
Jervis, Nelson do
Kalts, Jno. M. do
Kays, M. R. do
Kays, Jno. T. do
Kinney, Geo. do
Kinney, Hartman do
Kinney, Chaney do
Kinney, Jacob do
Kimball, Geter do
Koyt, Sylvester do
Kyte, Asa W. do
Lantz, Wm. do
Larow, Jno. B. do
Larow, Alex. do
Litts, Martin do
Losey, Jacob do
Mackerley, Chas. do
Mackerley, Wm. do
Mackerley, J. B. do
Mackerley, do
Mabee, Edward, do
Mabee, Simean do
Mabee, Martin, do
Mabee, Austin do
McPeek, Isaac do
McRoy, John do
Mead, Wm. H. do
Monroe, David do
Morris, Jno. D. do
Morris, Andrew do
Myers, Edward M. do
Nixon, Valentine do
Ousted, John do
Ousted, John, Jr., do
Owens, John C. do
Peters, Henry do
Pollinson, Wm. M. do
Price, Henry do
Prichard, H. do
Prichard, Wm. do

Quick, Geo.	Lafayette	States, L. J.	Lafayette
Quick, Wm. C.	do	Stephens, N. L.	do
Roe, Alex.	do	Stephens, Elisha	do
Roe, Amzi	do	Teabout, Anthony	do
Roland, Wm.	do	Teabout, John	do
Ross, W. J.	do	Terwilliger, Jas. J.	do
Sexton, Geo.	do	Thornton, Chas.	do
Shotwell, Samuel	do	Thornton, Geo.	do
Shuster, Jacob	do	Thompson, Jas.	do
Sharp, Morris	do	Thomas, R. T.	do
Sigler, John P.	do	Thomas, Ellis	do
Simmons, Jno.	do	Tidaback, Michael	do
Simmons, F.	do	Titus, Wm.	do
Simmons, Isaac A.	do	Vanblarcony, Garret,	do
Simmons, Wm.	do	Vanblarcom, Jos.	do
Simmons, Jacob	do	Vaughan, Jacob S.	do
Simonson, Wm.	do	Vaughan, Richard	do
Slater, Wm. L.	do	Van Netten, John	do
Slater, Jas.	do	Vought, Jos. V.	do
Slater, Sylvester	do	Warbass, Vincent	do
Smith, John	do	Warbass, Samuel	do
Snyder, John	do	Warbass, John	do
Snyder, Wm.	do	Ward, Geo. N.	do
Snyder, Raymond	do	Ward, Chas. R.	do
Snook, David C.	do	Weller, Wm.	do
Snook, Jacob, Jr.	do	Weller, John	do
Snook, Robt. G.	do	Williams, Josiah	do
Snook, Wm C.	do	Williams, Wm.	do
Snook, Peter	do	Williams, Elas	do
Space, Wm. O.	do	Winternante, O. B.	do
Space, Clark	do	Winters, Daniel	do
Struble, Amos	do	Woodward, J. B.	do
Struble, Geo. G.	do	Yetman, Eseek	do
States, A. P.	do	Yetman, Wm.	do

CHURNING MACHINES.

COLLVER & HUSTON,

In returning their grateful acknowledgments for past favors, would inform their numerous friends, and the public generally, that they are manufacturing and will constantly keep on hand for sale, their best Improved

ENDLESS CHAIN CHURNING MACHINES,

which they will sell on reasonable terms. The improvements to regulate the motion of the Churns while running, is something that every one keeping a Dairy should understand, before buying of any one else, and to meet the constantly improving taste of the public, they have been getting up a new set of patterns for a new style Dog Machine, which they will sell cheap.

We earnestly solicit the patronage of the community, and invite purchasers to come and bestow upon our work the most rigid inspection. Also, seasoned Cogs, such as are generally used for mill and other gearing, Leather and Rubber Belting, Circular Wood Saw Machines, Bark Mills, Corn Crackers, Cider Screws, Patent Mill Stone Bushes, Step Boxes, Improved Smut Machines, with Separation combined, for cleaning Grain. Also, the

American Turbine Water Wheels,

and all kinds of Mill Gearing fitted up to order.

COLLVER AND HUSTON,

LAFAYETTE, Sussex Co., N. J.

MONTAGUE TOWNSHIP.

Aber, Dennis, Hainesville
Aber, Eli, Brick House
Adams, Wm., Libertyville
Armstrong, Robt., Brick House
Armstrong, George, do
Auter, Jas. do
Auter, Jno. do
Ayers, B., Port Jervis, N. Y.
Bartlow, Wm. D., Brick House
Bennet, Jas. do
Bedell, Halsa do
Bonnell, Hon. Isaac, do
Brink, Andrew do
Brink, Nelson do
Brink, Peter do
Brink, Enos do
Brink, Jacob do
Bross, Eliakim do
Brown, A., Port Jervis, N. Y.
Bugsbee, Dan'l, Hainesville
Burrow, Stephen, Brick House
Burrous, Wm.,H. do
Buchanan, G. Port Jervis, N. Y.
Buchanan, Henry do
Camel, Horace, Brick House
Carman, Jos. do
Conklin, Jos. do
Cortwright, Sam'l do
Cortwright, Jacob do
Cortwright, Geo. do
Cortwright, Jno. do
Cole, Thomas V. do
Cole, Martin do
Cole, Jas. E. do
Cole, Jas., Jr., do
Cole, Jas. do
Cole, Wm. do
Cole, Joshua do
Cole, Jason do
Cole, Benj. H., do
Cole, Nelson L. do
Cole, Wm. H. do
Cole, Moses do
Cole, Solomon, Brick House
Coykendall, W. S., do
Coykendall, A. J., dc
Crowell, John do
Crowell, Geo. do
Crowell, S. V. do
Custard, Cyrus do
Custard, F. M. do
Davis, Geo. H. do
Davenport, H., Pt. Jervis, N. Y.
Decker, Wm. H., Brick House
Decker, Seely do
Dillistin, S. K. do
Everitt, Allen do
Everitt, Wm. C. do
Everett, Daniel D. do
Feasler, Jas. do
Fredericks, J. R., Port Jervis
Fuller, E. L. do
Fuller, Jas. E. do
Fuller, Jason, Brick House
Goddard, G., Port Jervis, N. Y.
Goucher, Benj., Brick House
Harden, Wm. do
Hawkins, Hiram do
Hornbeck, Jacob do
Hornbeck, Wm. P. do
Hornbeck, Benj. do
Hornbeck, Jas. do
Hornbeck, Isaac do
Hornbeek, Jos. S. do
Hornbeck, Geo. Y. do
House, Peter A. do
House, Daniel do
Hutchings, A. B., Port Jervis
Keller, Henry, Brick House
Knight, Annrew C. do
Kyte, John do
Labar, Wm. do
Lambert, Jas. do
Lambert, Jas., Jr. do
Lambert, H. do
Larow, Whitfield do

Lawrence, F., Pt. Jervis, N. Y.
Lawrence, Dan'l do
Lawson, J. A., Hainesville
Lawson, Jacob, do
Lawson, Samuel do
Lawson, Isaac do
Lawson, Wash. do
Little, E., Brick House
Little, Alonzo do
Litts, Edward do
Lundy, Jesse do
Lundy, Amos do
Lundy, Isaac do
Mandeville, A., Pt. Jervis, N.Y.
Mandeville, Jos. H. do
Mandeville, Francis do
Mandeville, G. H. do
Martin, Nathaniel do
Mead, David do
Middaugh, Ira do
Milligan, Lewis do
Morris, Samuel do
Nearpass, John do
Nearpass, S. do
Nearpass, Wm. do
Nyce, J. W., Brick House
Olden, Peter do
O'Grady, John do
Owens, Wm. do
Paugh, Peter do
Peach, Peter do
Perry, Geo. do
Perry, Alma T. do
Perry, Thomas do
Perry, Lancy do
Predmore, D. H. do
Price, Guy do
Quick, Jno. V. do
Rasor, R. do
Rasor, Fred'k K. do
Robeson, D., Port Jervis, N. Y.
Robeson, Joseph do
Robeson, Robert do
Romer, David, Brick House
Romer, Jacob do
Romer, Jno., Brick House
Rutan, Martin, Libertyville
Rutan, Jas. do
Saunders, J. D., Brick House
Schoonover, Joel do
Schoonover, W. H. do
Shimer, Joseph do
Shimer, Jacob do
Shimer, Jacob, Jr. do
Shimer, Albert do
Smith, A., Port Jervis, N. Y.
Smith, Isaac J. do
Smith, A. B., Brick House
Smith, Obadian do
Smith, Horace do
Stempest, Peter do
Storms, Silas, Pt. Jervis, N. Y.
Sydam, Silas, Brick House
Terwillager, M. do
Terwillager, L. M. do
Townsend, Amos do
Topping, J. W. Pt. Jervis, N. Y.
Utter, Isaiah, Brick House
Van Anken, Martin, do
Van Anken, J. S. do
Van Anken, J. T. do
Van Anken, Moffat do
Van Anken, H., P't Jervis, N. Y.
Van Anken, R. do
Van Etten, H. do
Van Etten, Levi, Brick House
Van Etten, Jos. do
Van Gordon, John do
Van Noy, Jos. do
Van Noy, J. J. do
Van Noy, Abram do
Van Noy, Aaron do
Van Noy, Jno. W. do
Vansickle, A. J., Libertyville
Wainright, W., Brick House
Wainright, Geo. do
Weed, Albert S. do
Weider, S. do
Westbrook, Lancey do
Westbrook, D. E. do

Westbrook, F.A.L.	Brick House	Westfall, S. J.,	Brick House
Westbrook, Alex.	do	Whalen, Michael	do
Westbrook, B. A.	do	Whitaker, Wm.	do
Westbrook, Geo. D.	do	Whiting, Jos.	do
Westbrook, M. V.	do	Wieland, G.	do.
Westbrook, Titus	do	Wilson, John	do
Westbrook, C. H.,	Port Jervis	Wireman, Jacob	do
Westfall, Geo. W.	do	Winters, S. C.,	Port Jervis, N.Y.
Westfall, David	do	Young, Peter,	Brick House
Westfall, Wilhelm	do		

NEWTON TOWNSHIP.

Newton Post Office.

Allen, E. M.
Ammerman, David
Anderson, Joseph
Anderson, Watson
Anderson, Wesley
Anderson, D. S.
Anderson, F. F.
Anderson, Thos.
Arvis, Chas.
Arvis, Theo.
Aspel, W. H.
Atno, Jas.
Barnes, B. A.
Babbit, Wm.
Bardsford, Thos.
Barrett, Myron
Baughan, Robt.
Baughan, J. M.
Baughan, Wm.
Baughan, Geo.
Barker, C. E.
Banaghan, Jno.
Beach, T. B.
Beach, Wm.
Beemer, J. S.
Beck, Lewis J.
Bennet, N. B.
Berry, Andrew
Bird, Abram
Bigler, Ira S.
Blanchard, Israel
Blanchard, Artimus
Blackwell, Elijah
Bonnell, Chas. M.
Bonnell, A. H.
Bonnell, H. C.
Both, John
Both, Joseph
Both, Alpheus
Boyd, Matthew
Boyler, Nicholas
Booth, J. R.
Bryant, Jacob
Brittin, Pemberton
Briggs, Allison
Bross, H. D.
Bross, Peter
Brown, R. H.
Brewer, John
Brewster, Jas.
Brewster, Edw.
Braisted, E. G.
Bunnell, T. G.
Burnhard, A.
Byington, T. L.
Case, Timothy
Case, E. L.
Campbell, Wm.
Campbell, Wm., 2d
Campbell, John
Campbell, Jason
Cannon, Peter
Cannon, Coulter
Casterline, W. D.
Cawley, Wm.
Cazim, Jos.
Calvin, John
Chandler, Jos.
Clark, Thos.
Clark, H. C.
Clark, Wm.
Clouse, Jos.
Cook, S. S.
Coon, Thos.
Couse, David, jr.
Coursen, S. J.
Couley, Merence
Cory, Perry
Cochran, Dennis
Cochran, Benj.
Cochran, Lewis
Conklin, Walter
Conklin, Albert
Conklin, A

Connell, Owen
Coult, Jos.
Coit, Chas.
Crook, Chas.
Criger, Wm.
Criger, Jas. W.
Craig, Jno. T.
Cummins, Geo.
Daly, Jas.
Davison, S. B.
Davison, Geo.
Davenport, Lucius
Davenport, Lewis
Dalson, Chas.
Daire, Amand
Decker, J. W.
Decker, P. S.
Demerest, Jas.
Devana, Patrick
Divers, J. E.
Dildine, Henry
Dillar, John
Dickerson, G. W.
Dickerson, M. D.
Drake, I. H.
Drake, G. M.
Drake, Martin
Drake, Wm.
Drake, J. B.
Drake, Archibald
Dunn, S. C.
Dunn, Jas.
Dunn, Lewis
Dunning, G. B.
Duncan, D. L.
Dunlap, Henry
Earl, Francis
Earl, Wm.
Earl, Benj.
Earls, Heatly
Earls, John
Earls, Geo.
Eberhart, Jos.
Edgarton, Justice
Edwards, Jas. A.
Edwards, John J.
Elston, Thos.
Emmons, Wm.
English, Jas.
English, John
Evert, Thos.
Ewald, Chas.
Farrell, Timothy
Farrell, Thos.
Farrell, Michael
Fellows, A. F.
Ferguson, Wm.
Finagan, Chris.
Foster, D. L.
Foster, R. E.
Foster, C. K.
Fox, Jas.
Fox, Wm.
Fox, A. H.
Fox, John
Frace, Michael
Frace, George
Fraukenwitz, S.
Freeman, A.
Garrison, P. L.
Garrison, G. B.
Gibson, J. S.
Gillam, J. W., jr.
Gilteland, Jno.
Givens, S. F.
Goldenburg, David
Gottschie, Aug.
Goodman, Rich'd.
Gordon, Jno. A.
Gould, Jacob
Gray, John
Gray, Francis
Gretzing, Jacob
Grover, Jacob
Grover, Edward
Hamilton, Robert
Hawk, Lewis
Hand, Benjamin
Harden, George
Hawkey, Richard
Hallock, I. C.
Harvey, Thomas
Havens, Jonathan
Haftner, Lewis
Hankenson, Jacob
Hankenson, John
Hendershot, Jos.
Hemenway, John
Heater, Wm.
Heater, John
Hess, Emerick
Hiles, Thos.
Hiles, Jacob
Hill, Joseph
Hill, John S.
Hill, Wm.
Hill, Enos
Hill, Silvester,
Howell, Seeley
Howell, John S.
Howell, George
Howell, John C.
Howell, John E.
Hoppaugh, Peter
Hough, Frank
Hough, Lester
Hogan, Roger
Hockenbury, A. B.
Hockenbury, C. E.
Hull, David R.
Hull, Geshum
Hull, Wm.
Hues, Martin
Hyder, Frances
Ike, Henry
Iliff, George
Iliff, John
Johnson, Samuel
Johnson, A. W.
Johnson, Robt. T.
Julier, George
Kays, Thos.
Kays, Thos., jr.
Kerr, David
Kent, Timothy

Kerns, Thomas
Kerns, John
Kensilla, W.
Kenner, Asa
Kenner, James
Kenney, Patrick
Kemble, Jacob
Kelsey, W. S.
Kintner, Martin
Kidney, Jas.
Kimball, Edwd.
Knox, A.
Knox, Peter
Knox, Benj.
Konkle, Israel
Konkle, A. H.
Koisting, Henry
Kraber, John
Kreonline, Frank
Laurence, Jacob
Lane, John W.
Lane, Clarkson E.
Lane, Chas.
Lane, Asa W.
Layton, Wm.
Landen, A. J.
Langer, Wm.
Laing, Oscar
Lamer, Conrad
Lewis, Jas. W.
Lewis, Jesse W.
Lewis, Freeman
Leport, Wm.
Leport, George R.
Lent, George W.
Leamer, Fred'k
Litts, Lemmerman
Lockwood, D. C.
Losey, Harris W.
Logas, Fred'k
Lose, Abram
Lyons, Jas.
Mason, Thomas
Matthews, Wm.
Matthews, James
Massaker, Lewis
Messaker, Henry L.
Messaker, John
Margarum, Theo.
Maddison, Wm. R.
Mattis, Wm.
Maloy, Thos.
Markaret, Julius
Meachum, Nathan
Mervill, E. V. W.
Miller, Wm.
Miller, Levi D.
Miller, Wm. S.
Mills, Thomas
Moore, Edward C.
Moore, Ira C.
Moore, John
Morford, Theodore
Morris, Richard
Mohare, Michael
Mohare, Thomas
Moffat, W.
Moran, Edward
Murphy, Martin
Myers, Chas.
Myers, Wallace
Myers, A.
McCollum, Moses
McCollum, Chas.
McCarty, Wm.
McCarter, Jno.
McCarter, H.
McCollum, C. J.
McCoskey, Edw.
McCormick, Jno.
McCluskey, John
McCoy, John
McGovern, Pat'k
McGovern, Mich'l
McGarvey, Pat'k
McGarvey, John
McMurtry, Wm.
McMayon, John
Newman, J. S.
Nelden, G. H.
Nelden, Geo.
Nichols, Wm. P.
Nichols, Henry
Nichols, Sam'l
Nixon, Hezekiah
Northrup, Jas.
Nolen, Augustus
Nolen, Wm.
Ogden, E.
O'Hara, S.
O'Leary, And'w
O'Leary, Redman
O'Neal, Pat'k
Parson, Nelson
Paugh, Lewis
Pellet, O. B.
Pellet, Obadiah
Pettet, R. M.
Pettet, Amos
Perrine, Wm.
Pinkney, Merret
Pierson, L. H.
Pool, Joseph
Price, A. W.
Price, Jas.
Price, Theo. N.
Prulet, Theo.
Quick, Albert
Quinn, Michael
Randoff, R. F.
Randle, Wesley
Ragan, Michael
Ramsden, Robt.
Reeves, O. D.
Richardson, W. J.
Rinker, Henry
Ridgway, Allen
Roe, Chas.
Roe, Chas. jr.
Rorbach, C. P.
Rosenkrans, Martin
Rosenkrans, L. D.
Roberts, S. P.
Rogers, Fred'k
Rose, Joseph
Ross, Wm. E.
Roy, Aaron N.
Roy, Joseph D.

Rudd, H. J.
Ryerson, Thos.
Ryerson, Martin
Sayre, David M.
Savercool, Wm'
Searls, Wm.
Sheeler, Abram
Shiner, Andrew
Shiner, John C.
Shiner, M. R.
Shiner, Chas.
Shafer, Jos. S.
Shafer, S. H.
Shafer, Abram
Shaw, Geo. C.
Shaw, Andrew
Shephard, Levi
Shoup, Malen
Shutz, T.
Sheppard, R. A.
Shotwell, Oscar
Simonson, A. J.
Simonson, T. F.
Sidner, Joel
Simmons, J. D.
Simpson, Henry
Simpson, E. I.
Slater, Jos. S.
Smith, J. W.
Smith, D. W.
Smith, Geo. T.
Smith, Geo. L.
Smith, Jas. L.
Smith, Chas.
Smith, Jas.
Smith, Merrian
Smith, Nelson
Smith, Franklin
Smith, Thos.
Smith, Franklin, jr.
Smaly, John S.
Snyder, John
Snyder, Jacob
Snyder, Martin
Squinton, Joseph
Stoll, H. C.
Stoll, Jackson
Stoll, John
Stewart, John T.
Stewart, Thos.
Stewart, Ira B.
Stewart, Benj.
Stuart, John R.
Struble, Ludwig
Stickles, David
Stickles, Chas.
Stackhouse, E. O.
Stackhouse, J. E.
Stells, J. W.
Step, Henry
Stanton, Patrick
Steel, Chas. N.
Steel, Daniel
Steel, W. D.
Sutton, L. H.
Sutton, R. F.
Sutton, Wm.
Swanbury, S.
Sweny, Thos.
Taylor, Wm. E.
Teel, Chester
Terry, Uriah
Thompson, Joseph
Thompson, Wm.
Thompson, David
Townsend, P. J.
Townsend, C.
Townsend, H. F.
Tomilty, Laurence
Truax, Geo. A.
Trusdall, Ladner
Trusdall, Wesley
Trusdall, L. H.
Traynor, Byran
Trelume, J. A.
Tuttle, R.
Tully, Michael
Tumith, James
Van Anken, B.
Van Blarcum, L.
Van Blarcum, A.
Van Campen, Wm.
Van Campen, S. J.
Van Campen, Benj.
Van Derbeck, Jas.
Van Etten, L. F.
Van Gelder, H.
Van Horn, G.
Van Horn, M.
Van Horn, A.
Van Sant, N.
Van Sant, Fred'k
Van Sickle, P. A.
Van Sickle, Peter
Van Voy, Chas.
Vernon, Alva
Vernon, W. H. R.
Ward, H. M.
Ward, Jesse
Ward, Patrick
Ward, Martin
Ward, Michael
Warbass, Ed.
Warbass, Jos.
Warner, Horace
Walker, W. H.
Walker, Geo. A.
Walker, Wm. A.
Wardell, Henry
Wheeler, Jno. T.
Witt, John
Wintermute, F. C.
Wintermute, R. S.
Winans, Chas.
Wilson, D. W.
Wilson, John
Williams, Jno. C.
Woodward, W. W.
Woodruff, Job
Woodruff, S. D.
Woodruff, Chas.
Woodruff, Moses
Woodruff, Stephen
Woodford, O. P.
Yarnell, John
Zebriskey, John
Zehan, Phillip

SANDYSTON TOWNSHIP.

Aber, Robert, Hainesville
Aber, Benj., Bevans
Arnst, Jas. D., Laytons
Ayres, Harrison do
Ayres, Israel, Tuttle's Corner
Banker, Jeremiah, Layton's
Bell, Peter, Hainesville
Bell, Benton do
Bell, Jesse do
Bell, John do
Bell, A., Tuttle's Corner
Bennett, N., Tuttle's Corner
Bevans, Jas. C., Bevans
Bevans, Daniel, Laytons
Bevans, Dayton do
Bevans, Robert do
Bevans, Solomon do
Bevans, Victor do
Bevans, John do
Bevans, Emmet, Hoinesville
Bevans, Benjamin R. do
Bevans, Obadiah do
Bevans, Evan, Laytons
Bevans, Sidney do
Bevans, N. do
Bevans, John J. do
Bevans, Wm. L. do
Bevans, Abraham do
Broadhead, C., Tuttle's Cor.
Brown, Jas. T., Bevans
Booth, Andrew, Laytons
Booth, Samuel, do
Bunn, S. M., Tuttle's Cor.
Bunn, Fred'k do
Bunn, Sam'l M. do
Cramer, John, Hainesville
Cramer, J. B. do
Cramer, A. B., Laytons
Cramer, Mathias do
Cramer Daniel, Hainesville
Clark, Samuel do
Clark. John Y. do
Clark, A. W., jr. do
Clark, A. W., Laytons
Clark, Wm. do
Clark, James do
Clark, Wm., jr. do
Conkling, Wm. do
Conkling, A. J., Hainesville
Conkling, Peter do
Conkling, Jacob do
Conkling, Samuel do
Conkling, John do
Conkling, Silas do
Coss, Elias, Bevans
Coss, Sam'l, Hainesville
Compton, John, Tuttle's Cor.
Compton, Wm. do
Compton. Joseph, Laytons
Coursen, J. E., Tuttle's Cor.
Cronk. Peter, Laytons
Cole, Jackson, Laytons
Crim, John, Montague
Creviling, J. L., Tuttle's Cor.
Creviling, H. E., Laytons
Cylcox, Joseph, Tuttle's Cor.
Depew, C., Hainvesville
Depew, R. do
Depew, M. E. do
Depew, Nelson do
Depew, A. O., Laytons
Depew, Elisha do
Depew, G. W. do
Depew, J. S. do
Decker, Alpheus, Bevans
Decker, John, Hainesville
Decker, Jas., Laytons
Decker, Edw. do
Decker, J. C., Hainesville
Degroat, Peter do
Degroat, John do
Dimon Alfred, Bevans
Dickson, Thos. do
Down. Rusling, Laytons
Drake, Peter do
Drake, Azariah, Hainesville

Drake, A., Hainesville
Drake, J., jr., Laytons
Drake, Benj. do
Drake, M. F., Tuttle's Cor.
Drake, John, Laytons
Drake, Wm. A., Hainesville
Dusenberry, E. A., Laytons
Dusenberry, Wm. do
Ellet, Abram, Tuttle's Cor.
Ellet, H. M. do
Ennes, Dan'l, Laytons
Everett, R. H. do
Everitt, J. D., do
Fleming, Joseph do
Fleming, Edward do
Fuller, Eli, Hainesville
Graw, Aug., Tuttle's Cor.
Graw, Henry, Laytons
Gumaur, Geo. Hainesville
Gumaur, H. do
Gumaur, G. H, do
Hartrim, John do
Henry, Geo. do
Hotalen, Jacob do
Hotalen, Sam'l do
Hotalen, John, do
Hotalen, W., Laytons
Hopler, Henry do
Hornbeck, B. E., Tuttle's Cor.
Hursh, B. D., Laytens
Hursh, W. C. do
Hursh, J. S., Hainesville
Huffman, Jas , Laytons
Jagger, B. W., Hainesville
Jagger, Anson do
Jagger, J. S, do
Johnson, A., Laytons
Kays, Jas. do
Kays, A., Tuttle's Cor.
Kittle, M. do
Kittle, Jos. do
Kief, D. do
Kintner, A. R., Hainesville
Kimer, C. F., Hainesville
Kyte, Thos., do
Kyte, Peter, Hainesville
Kyte, S. C. do
Kyte, Simeon do
Kyte, Peter, jr. do
Kyte, John do
Kyte, Ford do
Lattimore, D. B., Laytons
Layton, Francis do
Layton, Steward do
Layton, Edward do
Layton, William do
Layton, J. E., Tuttle's Corner
Lantz, Washington, Hainesville
Lanterman, John, do
Lanterman, James do
Lawson, Chester do
Leash, Amzi, Laytons
Losey, J. do
Losey, D., Tuttle's Corner.
Losey, A., Hainesville
Losey, A. C., do
Losey, Isaac do
Loder, S., Laytons
Lundy, Geo., Hainesville
Lundy, A, do
Major, Samuel do
Major, G. do
Major, J. V., Laytons
Merring, Jno. do
Merring, Geo. do
Merring, N. do.
Medan, Jacob do
Mettler, Benj. do
Myers, Peter, Hainesville
Myers, R. do
Myers, Robt. do
Myers, M. do
Myers, Geo. do
McManus, C. do
Newell, Wm., Hainesville
Newell, Wm., jr., do
Osborne, Wm., Laytons
Owen, E. T., Tuttle's Corner
Pitney, Leonard, Laytons
Pitney, Matthius do

Quick, John, Laytons
Quick, Joseph do
Quick, John, Hainesville
Raser, John do
Raser, Geo. do
Raser, Daniel do
Rechenbaugh, H. do
Rechenbaugh, H. do
Rosenkrans, D. H. do
Rosenkrans, W.W. do
Rosenkrans, A. P., Laytons
Rosenkrans, A. do
Rosenkrans, J. do
Roe, Elias H. do
Rutan, John L. do
Rutan, G. W., Hainesville
Rutan, Edwin do
Rubert, Geo. do
Rubert, Henry, Laytons
Schooley, Jas., Peters Valley
Schooley, John do
Shay, T. E. do
Shay, C. B., Hainesville
Shay, T. do
Shay, G. D. do
Shay, J. C. do
Shay, M. T. do
Shay, J. do
Shay, W. W. do
Shay, Jesse, Tuttle's Corner
Shaff, Levi, Laytons
Shaff, Isaac do
Shaff, F., Peters Valley
Shupe, Ruben do
Shupe, D., Wallpack Centre
Shafer, Moses, Hainesville
Sigler, W. do
Sigler, Mark do
Sigler, Samuel do
Sigler, Wickham do
Sliker, Jacob, Tuttle's Corner
Smith, J. J., Peters Valley
Smith, Philip, Bevans
Smith, J. do
Smith, E. C. do
Smith, Allan, Laytons
Snook, J. C. do
Snook, Wm., Tuttle's Cor.
Snyder, John, Tuttle's Cor.
Snyder, John, jr., do
Snover, Chas., Laytons
Spangenburgh, G., Tuttle's Cr.
Spangenburgh, J. Laytons
Spangenburgh, T. F., Bevans
Spangenburgh, J. E. do
Stoll, A. S. do
Stoll, Geo., Laytons
Stoll, Robt. Tuttle's Corner
Stoll, J. M. Hainesville
Stackhouse, M. do
Struble, Gideon, Laytons
Struble, Israal, Bevans
Steffan, H. Tuttle's Corner
Transue, A. E., Bevans
Tillman, N. S. Hainesville
Tillman, Alfred, Laytons
Tuttle, Benj. do
Tuttle, Benj. F. do
Tucker, Wm. do
Tucker, Jas. Tuttle's Corner
Utter, Benj. do
Utter, Dan. do
Utter, C. A. do
Utter, A. do
Van Anken, A. Hainesville
Van Anken, J. P. Laytons
Van Anken, F. Hainesville
Van Etten, Emanuel do
Van Etten, Mackley, Laytons
Van Sickle, Geo. do
Van Sickle, W. H. do
Van Sickle, B. P., Bevans
Van Ness, Edwin, Hainesville
Van Ness, Wm. do
Warner, Peter D. do
Warner, Daniel do
Warner, Joseph do
Warner, John do
Warner, Henry do
Warner, L. C. Bevans

Warner, M. V. B., Bevans
Westbrook, T. Hainesville
Westbrook, J. J. do
Westbrook, Alex. do
Westbrook, J. do
Westbrook, Abram do
Westbrook, A. K. Tuttle's Cr.
Westbrook, Oscar, Hainesville
Westbrook, R. B. do
Westbrook, W., Hainerville
Westbrook, O. Tuttle' Corner
West, John do
West, Chas., Laytons
Williams, G. P. do
Wilson, H. I., Hainesville
Youngs, Redder do
Youngs, J. B., Bevans
Youngs, John do

SPARTA TOWNSHIP.

Names of Freeholders only.

Ackerson, J. D., Sussex Mills
Ackerson, Cyrus, Lafayette
Ackerson, David, do
Ackerman, Abram, Sparta
Adams, Robt. K. do
Barkman, L. L. do
Beardslee, Marcus do
Beardslee, Chas., Ogdensburg
Beatty, Geo. B., Sparta
Bouker, John do
Bouker, S. H. do
Boss, John do
Bowman, P., Ogdensburg
Bradbury, Benj., Sparta
Byram, S. S. do
Byram, Jas. do
Castmore, Wm. do
Case, Geo. B. do
Case, O. P. do
Cary, Jno. B. do
Chidister, Step'n do
Clark, Richd., Ogdensburg
Collins, John do
Congleton, M. M., Monroe Crs.
Cole, Joseph, Sparta
Cory, Job do
Current, T. W. do
Current, Elias, Ogdensburg
Current, A., Sussex Mills
Dallas, Geo. M., Sparta
Decker, Jas. L. do
Decker, John do
Dorman, N., Ogdensburg
Dunlap, W. A., Sparta
Dunlap, Jos. M. do
Durling, Jno. V. do
Durling, Chas. do
Earl, Wm. do
Easton, Frank C. do
Edsall, J. A., Ogdensburg
Ellet, Samuel, Sparta
Emmans, T. do
Fisher, S. M., Sparta
Fisher, G. B. do
Flanegan, J., Ogdensburg
Freeman, H. C., Sparta
Galligar, Cornelius do
George, John, Ogdensburg
Goble, Isaac, Sparta
Goble, Isaac, jr. do
Goble, M. do
Goble, A. do
Goble, O. do
Goble, M. T. do
Hammil, H. do
Hammil, Sam'l do
Hayward, S. B. do
Halsey, Zopher do

Hemmovor, R., Sparta
Hendershot, J. do
Henion, Sam'l, Ogdensburg
Henion, John, do
Hoppaugh, J. B. do
Hopkins, J. Monroe Corners
Hopkins, Wm., Sparta
Hurd, W. H. do
Hurd, Isaac do
Hunt, Jno. M., Monroe Corners
English, J. R., Monroe Corners
Johnson, J. C., Sparta
Johnson, W. E. do
Keepers, Jno. H. do
Keef, D. A. do
Kiney, D. C. do
Kiney, Jno. C. do
Kiney, David do
Kiney, H. H. do
Kiney, Phillip do
Kiney, Jacob do
Kimble, D. H. Monroe Crs.
Kimble, R. M., Ogdensburg
Lazier, David, Sparta
Lacy, Frank do
Lanterman, M., Ogdensburg
Lanterman, J. D. do
Lanterman, Wm., do
Lanterman, Peter do
Lantz, David H., Sparta
Lemington, John do
Little, E. Y. do
Littell, A W., do
Littell, L. H. do
Lozier, Rob't D., do
Locklaw, Henry do
Lozier, E., Ogdensburg
Lyon, Stephen, Sparta
Maines, Wm. H. do
Maines, Jas. do
Mabee, M. W. do
Mabee, J., Monroe Corners
Madden, E., Ogdensburg
Maxwell, R. do
Masker, Abram, Sparta

Mills, Robert, Sparta
Moore, H. H. do
Morris, J. L. do
Munson, J. L. do
McCarty, Jas. do
McCarty, Laur'ce do
McDavit, S. do
McDavit, Thos. do
McEntee, M., Ogdensburg
McGuire, Jas. do
McPeek, Rich'd, Sparta
McPeek, D. S, Monroe Crs.
Newman, T., Ogdensburg
Nichols, Ziba, Sparta
Norman, Chas. do
Norman, Robt. do
Norman, Wm. do
Norman, Peter, Ogdensburg
Oliver, S., Lafayette
Orsborne, Isaac, Sparta
Orsborne, J. do
Pierson, D. Y. do
Pierson, Able do
Pierce, Anthony, Ogdensburg
Polly, Alva, Sparta
Predmore, W. J., Ogdensburg
Pullis, David, Sparta
Reed, Geo. do
Regan, C., Ogdensburg
Riker, John J., Sparta
Riker, John S. do
Riker, Millage do
Richards, John do
Rochell, Stephen do
Rockett, P., Ogdensburg
Rosenkrans, J., Lafayette
Ross, John, Sparta
Sanford, Collins do
Sheldon, John, do
Shuman, J. H. do
Sickles, Wm. do
Slockbower, F. M. do
Smith, Dan'l do
Smith, Rich'd R. do
Smith, Sam'l, Ogdensburg

Mackerly, M., Ogdensburg
Struble, Jacob, do
Struble, G. M., Sparta
Staley, John, do
Stillwell, Dan'l do
Staneback, J. B. do
Strait, H. B. do
Stidworthy, E., Ogdensburg
Stidworthy, Thos., do
Sutton, G. M., Monroe Corners
Taylor, J. D., Ogdensburg
Thorp, Jas. do
Thorp, P. H. do
Tidaback, Daniel do
Timberel, Jacob, Sparta
Titman, J. B. do
Turner, Emanuel do
Underwood, R., Ogdensburg
Vaughn, John, Lafayette
Vaughn, Geo., Sparta
Van Blaricom, G., Monroe Crs.
Van Blaricom, G. S., Sparta
Van Bushkirk, J. M. do
Van Kirk, Thos. do
Van Kirk, Mills do
Washer, Robt. P. do
Washer, Peter do
Welsh, John, Ogdensburg
Whitford, Geo. do
White, Jno. L., Sparta
Wilson, Geo. O. do
Woodruff, John, do
Wright, B. H., Sussex Mills
Youngs, David, Sparta

STILLWATER TOWNSHIP.

Adams, Wm., Fredon
Andress, H. Middleville
Andress, Oscar, do
Andress, M., do
Angle, C. H. M., Stillwater
Anderson, Lewis, Middleville
Avery, Abram, do
Ayres, Geo., Swartswood
Bell, Uriah, do
Beemer, Philip
Bedell, Henry, Middleville
Beegle, Jno. S., Stillwater
Blackford, John, Middleville
Blackford, Sam'l, do
Blackferd, S. R., do
Blackford, Geo., do
Blackford. Wm., do
Blackford, Jno. W., do
Bloom, Jnõ. D., Stillwater
Brown, A. L., do
Butler, Jas., Middleville
Budd, Mahlon, Hunts Mills
Budd, Jno. S., do
Case, David, Swartswood
Canfield, Alford, Fredon
Chandler, Edw'd, Stillwater
Clauson, H. A., Swartswood
Clauson, A. W., Stillwater
Clouse, Jacob, Hunts Mills
Coursen, Jos. H., Stillwater
Coursen, Wm. P., Fredon
Cooke, L. I., Stillwater
Cooke, Geo., do
Cougleton, Elias, Swartswood
Condit, Rev. Sam'l, Stillwater
Condit, Elbert M., do
Condit, Isaac H., do
Cole, Harrison, Fredon
Cole, Jacob, do
Cole, Austin, do
Crouse, Geo. W., Stillwater
Crawn, Jacob, Swartswood
Crawn, Isaac, Middleville
Crawn, Jno. C., do
Crawn, Wm., de
Dangler, Sam'l, Stillwater
Decker, Aedrew, Fredon
Decker, Horace, do

Decker, Alvey, Fredon
Decker, Edw. S., Swartswood
Decker, Lewis, do
Decker, Thos., do
Devore, Peter, Middleville
Devore, Wm., do
Dennis, David W., Swartswood
Dennis, Jacob, Fredon
Dennis, M. R., Stillwater
Deats, Jonathan, do
Divers, Wm., Middleville
Divers, Jacob M., Stillwater
Divers, Christopher, do
Emons, Nehemiah, Fredon
Emons, H. L., do
Emons, Jacob, do
Emons, A. J., do
Emons, Jas., Swartswood
Emery, Jno., do
Emery, Cornelius, do
Emery, Nathaniel, do
Ervey, Jas. B., Stillwater
Fretz, Martin, do
Gariss, Geo. D., do
Gariss, John, do
Gray, Robt. M., Fredon
Grover, Robt. I., co
Grover, Jacob, Stillwater
Grover, Casper, do
Grover, Peter B., do
Grover, James, Swartswood
Goble, Elias R., Fredon
Goble, Roy, R., do
Gunterman, P. C., Stillwater
Harker, Jas. M., do
Hazen, John V., Hunts Mills
Hazen, Melville, do
Hazen, Jesse, Swartswood
Hardick, John W., Middleville
Hardick, Lemuel, do
Hardick, Nathaniel, do
Hardick, Isaac, do
Hardick, Wm. N., do
Hardick, S. A., Stillwater
Hammond, Isaac, Middleville
Hammond, And'w, Middleville
Hamler, Jas. A., Hunts Mills
Hendershot, Abm. Swartswood
Hendershot, John L., do
Hendershot, M., do
Hendershot, Henry N., do
Hendershot, Chauncey, do
Hendershot, Levi, do
Hendershot, A. J., do
Hendershot, J. L., do
Hibler, Jacob, do
Hill, P. S., Stillwater
Hill, N., do
Hill, S., do
Hill, John H., do
Hill, Simon, Swartswood
Hill, Baltis, do
Hill, George V., do
Hill, O., do
Hill, H. J., do
Hovey, Dan'l, Fredon
Hough, T., Swartswood
Hoagland, John, Hunts Mills
Huff, Geo. W., Stilllwater
Huff, Isaac, do
Huff Abram V., do
Huff, Dan'l, do
Huff, Isaac C., do
Huff, Jos. L., do
Huff, Henry D., do
Huff, Charles, do
Huff, Jos., do
Huff, George V., do
Huff, Henry, do
Huff, Austin, do
Huff, Andrew, Middleville
Huff, Joel W., do
Hull, Theo., Swartswood
Hunt, David, do
Hunt, Jos. O., do
Hunt, Alex., do
Hunt, Wm. O., Fredon
Hunt, John, do
Hunt, T. Middleville
Hunt, John W., Hunts Mills

Hunterdon, Thos., Swartswood
Kays, L. B., Middleville
Kays, John C., do
Keane, John W., do
Keane, Geo., do
Keane, Geo. W., do
Keane, Isaac, Swartswood
Kintner, Peter, Middleville
Kise, Isaac, Stillwater
Knox, Wm. M., do
Jarvis, Bethnel, do
Jones, Wm., do
Johnson, Steven, do
Johnson, David L., do
Johnson, Jas. M., do
Latermore, G. W., Swartswood
Lambert, Jos., Middleville
Lanning, David, Stillwater
Lanterman, J. T., do
Lemmons, Wm., Swartswood
Lewis, James, Stillwater
Lewis, Nathaniel, do
Linch, Matthew, Swartswood
Losey, Geo. W., Stillwater
Losey, A. N., do
Losey, Casper, do
Luse, Aaron, Hunts Mills
Maine, John S., Stillwater
Maine, Abram T., do
Maine, Henry S., do
Maine, Jacob D., do
Maine, John W., do
Maine, Abram, do
Maine, Wm., do
Maine, W. A., do
Maine, Elias D., do
Martin, Benj., Swartswood
Mackey, Philip, Stillwater
Marvin, D. B., Middleville
Merkel, Peter, Fredon
Mills, Ira, Swartswood
Morrison, Alex, Hunts Mills
Moore, Chas. V., Stillwater
Moore, Chas. H., do
Morris, Dan'l S., Fredon
Morris, Moses, Swartswood
Morris, Peter, do
Morris, Wesley, do
McDanalds, Hugh, do
McConnell, Wm., Stillwater
Nuagent, Thomas, do
Nuagent, John. do
Obdyke, John W., do
Obdyke, John S., do
Ogden Jos. C., Middleville
Ogden, A. N., do
Ogden, Philip, do
Ogden, George L., do
Oliver, Wm., Swartswood
Oliver, Matthew, do
Osmon, S. C., Fredon
Ozenbaugh, John, Middleville
Pittenger, N., Swartswood
Pittenger, F. S., do
Powers, Henry, Stillwater
Potter, Benj. A., do
Potter, Thos. A., do
Potter, Horace, do
Potter, Samuel, do
Preston, Samuel, do
Predmore, Garret, Swartswood
Predmore, J. C., do
Puder, Geo., Stillwater
Roy, Insley, do
Roy, Robert I., do
Roy, Chas., do
Roy, B., do
Roy, Chas. N., Middleville
Rosenkrans, G., Stillwater
Rosenkrans, Isaac, do
Rodgers, Henry, do
Roof, Jacob, J., Stillwater
Roof, Geo., W., do
Roof, Leonard, do
Roof, Christopher, do
Roof, John, Swartswood
Roof, Oliver, do
Roe, Wm.. T., Hunts Mills
Ryman, Geo., Stillwater
Savacool, J. N., do

Savacool, Alfred, Stillwater
Savacool, Geo. W., do
Savacool, N., do
Savacool, Geo. A., do
Savacool, Peter, do
Savacool, Jacob W., do
Savacool, A. R., Fredon
Savacool, J., do
Savacool, P. J., Swartswood
Savacool, Henry Middleville
Schoonover, A, Swartswood
Schoonover, Wm., do
Schooley, Evi B., Middleville
Shotwell, James I., Fredon
Shotwell, I., do
Shotwell, Geo. W., do
Shafer, Robert F., Stillwater
Shafer, Abram, E. do
Shaver, Peter, Fredon
Shaw, John, Hunts Mills
Shaw, Wm. H., do
Shuster, John, Stillwater
Shuster, Abram, do
Shired, Jesse, Swartswood
Siperley, C., Swartswood
Simmons, Jacob, Middleville
Skinner, Wm. E., Stillwater
Sliker, Andrew, Swartswood.
Sliker, Isaac, do
Sliker, John, do
Sliker, Wm., Stillwater
Smith, Barton, do
Smith, Wm., Fredon
Smith, Jos., "
Smith, Geo., "
Smith, John P., "
Smith, Jas. J., do
Snook, Jno. N., do
Snook, Jacob M,, do
Snover, J. S., Stillwater
South, Theo., Swartswood
South, Isaac, do
South, John, do
South, Edw'd, do
Southard, Wm., do
Southard, M. J., Swartswood
Struble, Britton, do
Struble, Alpheus, do
Struble, Joseph, do
Struble, Theo. F., Hunts Mills
Stickles, Z. M., Swartswood
Staley, A. J., do
Staley, George A., Middleville
Staley, John C., do
Staley, James H., do
Staley, H. A., do
Sutton, Theo., Stillwater
Swazey, D. R., Fredon
Swartswelder, Geo., Stillwater
Swartswelder, Jno., E. do
Swartswelder, M. H., do
Talmadge, Jno., Middleville
Thomson, Sam'l, do
Tindall, Jacob, Stillwater
Titman, B., Swartswood
Titman, Wm., do
Titman, W. H., do
Titman, Jos., do
Titman, Geo., do
Titman, B., Jr., do
Tunison, Tunis, Stillwater
Van Doren, A. J., Fredon
Van Horn, Philip, Middleville
Van Horn, Wm. H., do
Van Horn, Wm., do
Van Horn, Robert, do
Van Horn, J. L., do
Van Horn, Wm., Jr., do
Van Stone, Henry, Fredon
Van Stone, John, do
Van Dine, James, Middleville
Vought, Andrew, do
Vought, W., Fredon
Ward, Ezekiel, Middleville
Ward, Alfred, do
Ward, Alfred, Jr., do
Westbrook, Jno. A., do
Wilever, Philip, do
Wintermute, Wm., do
Wintermute, Rubin, Stillwater

Wintermute, John, Stillwater
Wintermute, J. A., do
Williams, Enos, Swartswood
Williams, Jas., do
Yetter, Simeon, Middleville
Yetter, Geo. L., do
Yetter, I. H., Middleville
Yetter, S., Jr., do
Yetter, George W., do
Yetter, Jacob do
Youmans, Benj., Stillwater
Youmans, M. J. W,. do

VERNON TOWNSHIP.

Acker, Edward, Vernon
Ackerson, Wm do
Allen, Carlos do
Allen, Wm., Deckertown
Arvis, Fred'k., Glenwood
Baxter, J. C. do
Baxter, John do
Baxter, Sharp, do
Baxter, Asa, Wawayanda
Barley, Fred'k, Deckertown
Barley, Joseph do
Barley, Estle do
Barley, Usual do
Babcock, Lewis do
Babcock, James do
Babcock, Abner do
Babcock, Joseph do
Babcock, T. L. do
Babcock, Wm. do
Babcock, Jacob do
Babcock, Isaac, Stockholm
Babcock, J. M. Wawayanda
Babcock, James do
Barrett, Wm., McAffee
Barrett, D., New Milford, N. Y.
Barrett, D., jr. do
Barrett, Gilbert do
Barrett, James E. do
Barrett, Wm. do
Belcher, Sylvester, Glenwood
Belcher, Jacob do
Belcher, Benj. do
Berry, J. J., Canisteer
Bishop, Abner, Wawayanda
Bissett, James, Deckertown
Bird, Wm. do
Birdsall, Henry, McAffee
Birdsall, Frederick do
Bloom, Albert, Glenwood
Bisdeck, Jas. E. do
Blanchard, Aaron, Vernon
Blanchard, Artemus, do
Booth, John, Deckertown
Boyce, Wm., Vernon
Boys, J. A., do
Boys, Wm. do
Boyd, R. A., Stockholm
Bowen, Arthur, Wawayanda
Bowen, Winfield do
Brown, P. J., Glenwood
Brown, J. A., Vernon
Brown, G. S. do
Brown, T. H., Wawayanda
Brant, Herman, McAfee
Brant, Wm., Wawayanda
Brion, R., Stockholm
Brion, W., Wawayanda
Brook, John, Deckertown
Buchanan, H. do
Burns, Dennis, Glenwood
Card, Israel, Wawayanda
Card, Wm., Stockholm
Card, Sylvester do
Card, John do
Card, John, jr. do
Card, Hyram do
Card, Daniel do
Card, Amzi, Wawayanda

Campbell, John, Vernon
Campbell, Wm. do
Campbell, H. K. do
Carpenter, J. S., Glenwood
Carr, J., New Milford, N. Y.
Carr, David do
Carr, Vincent do
Case, J. B., Glenwood
Chardavoyne, H., Vernon
Chardavoyne, Robt. do
Chardavoyne, J. W. do
Cole, Abram, Stockholm
Cooper, G., Wawayanda
Cooper, J. J., do
Cooper, Moses C. do
Cooper, Jno. do
Cooper, Wesley do
Conkling, J. S., Vernon
Conkling, J. S., jr. do
Conkling, P. C., Unionville, N.Y.
Conkling, Peter, Deckertown
Cook, R., Vernon
Cook, A. J., Glenwood
Cill, F., Stockholm
Crabtree, Wm., Vernon
Crabtree, John do
Crisey, J. D., Glenwood
Crum, Geo. do
Crist, Fred. do
Lramer, Peter, Vernon
Day, Albert, Stockholm
Day, J. L. do
Day, Christian do
Davison, J., Deckertown
Decker, Wm. H., Vernon
Decker, Joel do
Decker, Edw. do
Decker, John do
Decker, Lewis do
Decker, Philip, Deckertown
Denton, Rich., Vernon
Denton, Solomon, do
Dekay, Thos. do
Dekay, H. B. do
Dekay, John do
Dekay, T. S. Vernon
Dekay, Harrison do
Dekay, E. A. do
Dixon, David, Stockholm
Dixon, Wm. do
Dixon, J. C. do
Drew, Barnett, Vernon
Drew, S. L. do
Drew, J. S. do
Drew, Thos. do
Drew, Ira do
Drew, Samuel do
Drew, Wm. S. do
Drew, Gilbert do
Drew, Jas. K. do
Drew, E. W. do
Drew, Isaac do
Drew, Wm. M. do
Drew, Gilbert, 2d do
Drew, Peter do
Dunn, M. C., Deckertown
Edsall, David, Vernon
Edsall, Wm. do
Edsall, J. P. do
Edsall, Wm. R. do
Edsall, W. W. do
Edsall, Sidney do
Edsall, J. G. do
Edsall, Sam'l do
Eliot, Jas., Glenwood
Farber, John, Vernon
Farber, Wm. do
Farber, Israel do.
Farber, Amos do
Farber, Nicholas do
Fermer, Wm. do
Fermer, Maurice, Stockholm
Force, C., Vernon
Fogerson, Calvin, Deckertown
Fogerson, J. H., Stockholm
Fogerson, Freeman do
Frazy, Wm. do
Francisco, James, Vernon
Fuller, L. J. do
Garrison, John do

Garrison, Samuel, Vernon
Garrison, Jackson do
Gardenhouse, J. M. do
Gardenhouse, John do
Givans, J. F. do
Givans, N. V. do
Givans, John do
Givans, Samuel, Deckertown
Givans, Samuel, jr., Vernon
Gorton, Lorenzo do
Green, Jas. do
Green, W. W. do
Green, Geo. do
Green, J. H. do
Green, John do
Green, Robt., Wawayanda
Grinell, T. M., Glenwood
Grigary, J. G., Vernon
Grigary, Fred. do
Hamilton, Thos. do
Halwick, C., Glenwwod
Heedy, Hezekiah, do
Henderson, E., Vernon
Henderson, Jas. do
Heater, John do
Howell, Harrison do
Houston, Philip, Glenwood
House, Thos., Vernon
House, Thos., jr., do
Howard, Wm., Wawayanda
Holly, Wm., Vernon
Horton, Wallace, Wawayanda
Hovencamp, Wm., Glenwood
Hunt, Wm., Vernon
Hunt, Geo. do
Hunt, Norton do
Hunt, Lemuel do
Hunt, Wm. S. do
Huzzy, M., Wawayanda
Jay, Joseph, Deckertown
Jenkins, S., McAfee
Jenkins, John do
Jones, Edw. Deckertown
Jones, Zenes do
Jones, David do

Keyzer, Adam, Vernon
Kerren, S. Deckertown
Kieffer, Wm. R. Vernon
Kock, Wilhelm do
Lazier, Jacob do
Lazier, J. H. do
Layton, Samuel do
Limer, Jas. H. do
Little, J. V. Deckertown
Little, J. R. do
Little, Wm. S. do
Loot, J. S. do
Lott, John do
Lott, John, jr. do
Lott, B. S. do
Martin, E. A. Vernon
Martin, Wm. C. do
Martin, Jas. E. do
Martin, Jacob, Deckertown
Martin, Isaac do
Martin, Thos. do
Martin, Parkson do
Mapes, J. D., Vernon
Mabee, John, Stockholm
Mabee, Collins do
Mabee, Robt. do
Mann, Thos. A., Wawayanda
Mann, Thos. W., Vernon
Marshall, Aaron, Stockholm
Mills, John, Vernon
Mills, Wm. do
Mott, Wm. W., Deckertown
Morehouse, John, Glenwood
Morgan, Patrick, Wawayanda
Munson, David do
Munson, Berry do
Munson, Chas. do
Mulcry, Wm., Vernon
McCloud, D. O., Wawayanda
Newkirk, John, McAfee
Odell, Nath., Deckertown
Osborn, George, Vernon
Osborn, Albert do
Osborn, Ralph do
Osborn, John do

Osborn, H. W., Vernon
Osborn, Benj. do
Osborn, Albert 2d do
Owen, Wm., Unionville, N. Y.
Owen, J. E., McAfee
Parker, James, Vernon
Parker, Wm. do
Parker, Geo. do
Parker, A. do
Parker, A., jr. Glenwood
Parker, John do
Paddick, J. H., Wawayanda
Paddick, Snider do
Paddick, Sidney do
Paddick, Henry do
Paddick, Wm., Vernon
Paddick, Ebenezer do
Paddick, Isaac do
Paddick, J. H. do
Parks, Taylor, Deckertown
Parks, Nath., Vernon
Parks, Atkinson, Glenwood
Perrigo, S., Deckertown
Potter, E. Unionville, N. Y.
Potter, J. V. do
Predmore, D. A. Vernon
Predmore, J. L. Wawayanda
Predmore, Thos. M. do
Price, L. G. Vernon
Pullis, J. C. Wawayanda
Raymond, Jas. Vernon
Rhodes, Nelson, Glenwood
Rhodes, J. E. do
Rhodes, G. W. do
Riggs, Wm., McAfee
Riggs, J. A. do
Riggs, Horace do
Riggs, John do
Riggs, H. E. do
Riggs, David do
Rickey, Wm. Vernon
Risedeck, S. Glenwood
Roe, Wm., Unionville, N. Y.
Roberts, John, McAfee
Romer, John, Wawayanda
Romine, Jas., Wawayanda
Romine, Richard, Vernon
Romine, Abraham do
Rude, Sam'l K., McAfee
Rude, Abraham do
Rude, Spencer do
Rutan, Abraham, Vernon
Rutan, Henry do
Ryerson, Peter N. do
Ryerson, N. P., Deckertown
Ryerson, Paul T., Vernon
Sammis, Henry, Deckertown
Sammis, Joseph do
Sammis, Isaac do
Scofield, A. do
Sealy, Wm. H., Vernon
Selmes, S., Wawayanda
Serles, Wm., Vernon
Shaw, Wm. H. do
Shelley, Sam'l, Deckertown
Simonson, Wm., McAfee
Simonson, C., Vernon
Simonson, Jos., do
Simpson, Smith, McAfee
Simpson, Wm. do
Simpson, Robt. do
Simpson, J. E., Vernon
Smith, Wm., McAfee
Smith, Alanson do
Smith, Benj. do
Smith, Wm. jr. do
Smith, John, Vernon
Smith, Adam, Stockholm
Smith, A. C. do
Smith, Theo. do
Smith, Geo., Vernon
Smith, J. W. do
Snider, Oliver, Wawayanda
Snider, Isaac do
Sprague, Ebenezer, Vernon
Sprague, Samuel do
Sprague, Gilbert do
Sprague, Josiah do
Sprague, Randle, McAfee
Sprague, J. G. do

Springer, Horace, Vernon
Springer, L. do
Strater, Wm., McAfee
Straight, Theo., Stockholm
Stormes, Horace, Vernon
Stormes, J. J. do
Stormes, Silas do
Strait, B. R., Stockholm
Strait, J. S. do
Strait, Wm. A. do
Sulivan, Michael, Wawayanda
Taylor, Jas. E., Vernon
Taylor, Wm. J. do
Terwiliger, Oscar, Glenwood
Thornton, J. S., Deckertown
Toland, Abner, Glenwood
Toland, Lewis do
Toland, Wm. do
Utter, J. M., Stockholm
Utter, H. S. do
Utter, Wm. do
Van Nostrand, J. L., Glenw'd
Van Nostrand, Theo. do
Van Winkle, Wm. do
Van Houten, J. S. D'kertown
Van Houten, A., Stockholm
Van Gilder, I. R., Glenwood
Van Winkle, Jno. do
Van Riper, T. H., Vernon
Vanderhoof, J., Deckertown
Vanderhoof, A. do
Vail, John, Glenwood
Vealy, Evi, Glenwood
Vealy, J. H. do
Walling, Francis, Vernon
Warr, D. D., N. Milford, N. Y.
Walde, Thos., Glenwood
Ward, Rich., do
Webb, Jas. E., Vernon
Webb, Wm. H. do
Webb, Austin do
White, Hezekiah do
Winans, H. K. do
Williams, J. A. do
Williams, Isaac do
Williams, Wm. H. Stockholm
Williams, Frank do
Williams, Joseph do
Wilcox, Horace, McAfee
Winters, J. W., Wawayanda
Winters, Isaac, Vernon
Worry, J. W. do
Wood, Geo. J. do
Wood, Jas. R. do
Wood, J. A. do
Wood, Stephen H. do
Wood, Theo. F. do
Wright, S. C., McAfee
Wright, Wm. do
Yancy, Lawrence, Vernon
Yeomans, J. N. do
Youngs, Benj., Stockholm
Youngs, Jacob do

WALLPACK TOWNSHIP.

Berk, Jno., Wallpack Centre
Bevans, Alfred do
Bell, Robt. do
Bell, S. W. do
Bush, Daniel do
Buss, David, Flatbrookville
Bunnell, David do
Cisco, H. N. do
Cisco, Robt. do
Clark, Jesse, Wallpack Centre
Cole, Dayton do
Cole, Oliver, Flatbrookville
Cole, Benj. do
Cole, J. S. do
Darrohn, R. S. do
Decker, Calvin do
Decker, Moses do
Decker, Simeon do

Decker, Martin, Flatbrookville
Decker, D. D. do
Decker, J. S. do
Decker, Wm. do
Dickerson, M. do
Dickerson, J. do
Dickerson, R. T. do
Dickerson, Geo do
Dickson, S. Wallpack Centre
Drake, W. C„ Flatbrookville
Earl, Wm. do
Earl, Simeon do
Fuller, Jno. B. do
Fuller, Jas. W. do
Fuller, O. do
Fuller, B. D. do
Gariss, Fred'k do
Gariss, Peter do
Gariss, Jacob do
Gariss, Elias do
Gariss, J. W. do
Gariss, P. J. do
Gariss, John do
Gariss, S. H. do
Gariss, I., Wallpack Centre
Gariss, J. W., Jr., do
Gariss, S. J. do
Gunn, C. D. do
Gunn, Christopher do
Haney, Chas., Flatbrookville
Haney, Josiah do
Halstead, I. D., Wallpack Cr.
Hill, Jason K., Flatbrookville
Hill, Ostrom do
Hill, A. H. do
House, J. P. do
Hornbeck, Jacob do
Hornbeck, Alex. do
Hornbeck, Peter do
Huff, W. C. do
Hull, Wm. do
Hull, Martin do
Hull, Gershom do
Hull, Jos. Wallpack Centre
Johnson, Enos do

Jones, Cyrus, Flatbrookville
Jones, A. J. do
Kishbaugh, Chas. do
Kishbaugh, Isaac do
Kishbaugh, Jacob do
Knight, D. Wallpack Centre
Knight, Elisha do
Knight, Albert, Flatbrookville
Labar, J. Wallpack Centre
Layton, R., do
Litts, S. R. Flatbrookville
Litts, C. H. do
Losey, David, Wallpack Cr.
Losey, John, do
Losey, John, jr. do
Losey, Cyrus do
Losey, Amos do
Losey, Benj. Flatbrookville
Marthis, Lewis A. do
Maines, D. E. do
Merrel, Elias M. Bevans
Merring, F. Wallpack Centre
Merring, Jacob do
Mitten, Horace do
Miller, Rev. Mr. do
Nyce, Jas. Flatbrookville
Petty, Peter P., Bevans
Pierce, Thos. Flatbrookville
Ramer, Thos. Bevans
Ribble, A. J. Wallpack Centre
Ribble, H. do
Roe, Jacob S. do
Roe, Thos. do
Robins, Jos. do
Rosenkrans, S. do
Rosenkrans, S., Flatbrookville
Rosenkrans, J. S. do
Rosenkrans, Benj. do
Rosenkrans, Elijah do
Rosenkrans, Avert do
Room, John do
Rundell, I. S., Wallpack Cr.
Schoonover, John do
Shay, Levi do
Sheets, Samuel, Bevans

Sigafuss, Wm. Flatbrookville,
Shupe, E. A., Flatbrookville
Smith, Jacob D. do
Smith, John S. do
Smith, S. D. do
Smith, Jonas do
Smith, Dan'l do
Smith, Dan'l S. do
Smith, Jacob do
Smith, J. K. do
Smith, F. do
Smith, S. D. 2d do
Smith, Martin do
Smith, Wm. Bevans
Smith, W. D. do
Snover, H. D. Flatbrookville
Snover, John do
Snover, Theo. do
Spangenburg, W. H. W'p'k Cr.
Stoll, Hudson, Wallpack Cen'e
Stoll, Oakley, do
Stoll, J. do
Stoll, Jackson, Flatbrookville
Tillman, N. Wallpack Centre
Trauger, E. E., Flatbrookville
Transue, M. M., Wallp'k Cr.
Transue, Hiram do
Van Auken, N. Flatbrookville
Van Auken, B. do
Van Auken, B. jr. do
Van Horn, Peter do
Van Horn, Abraham do
Van Horn, P. B. W'pack Cr.
Van Gordon, B. Flatbrookville
Van Why, John do
Winans, Theo. W'pack Cr.
Wood, J. H. do
Youmans, S. B., Bevans

WANTAGE TOWNSHIP.

Adams, J. E. Deckertown
Adams, V. do
Adams, P. do
Adams, Jas. do
Adams, Elijah do
Adams, Jas. R. do
Adams, J. E. jr. do
Adrian, A. Bemerville
Armstrong, T. Deckertown
Ayres, Wm., Libertyville
Ayres, Chandler do
Ayres, Levi do
Ayres, Enoch do
Ayres, David B. do
Ayres, E. D. do
Ayres, Jacob do
Ayres, Dayton do
Ayres, Geo. P. Coleville
Ayres, Evi B. do
Ayres, M. H. do
Ayres, Nelson, Libertyville
Ayres, G. W., Deckertown
Ayres, A. do
Babcock, John, Coleville
Baird, Nehemiah, Mt. Salem
Baird, D. E. do
Beattie, J. W. Deckertown
Belcher, B. do
Beemer, Harrison do
Beemer, J. H. do
Beemer, J. Hy. do
Beemer, J. E. do
Beemer, Hy., Beemerville
Beemer, J. M. do
Beemer, G. L. do
Beemer, Isaac, Libertyville
Beemer, Alva do
Beemer, J. W. do
Beemer, Hiram do
Beemer, Evi C. do
Beemer, Elias, Coleville
Beemer, J. C. do

Beemer, Levi, Coleville
Beemer, J. B. do
Berry, W. Deckertown
Berry, Britton do
Berry, Lewis do
Berry, Halsey do
Berry, John do
Berry, Wesley do
Bennet, E. P. do
Benjamin, D. W. do
Benjamin, S. do
Benjamin, S. W. Un'vlle, N. Y.
Bedell, L. S., Coleville
Bedell, Peter do
Bedell, A. Deckertown
Blair, Jacob, Hamburg
Bond, Nath. Deckertown
Bowman, John, Beemerville
Bowman, Wm. Libertyville
Bowman, D. Deckertown
Bowman, Walter do
Bowman, Web. do
Bowman, Fred., Coleville
Bowman, Jefferson do
Bowman, John do
Bowman, L. do
Bross, O. J. do
Bross, Peter do
Bross, O. L. do
Bross, A. V. do
Bross, Thos. do
Bross, Peter B. do
Bross, D. Unionville, N. Y.
Bross, Noah do
Bronson, Oscar, Deckertown
Bray, Thomas do
Brown, J. O. do
Braisted, Edward, Coleville
Brink, Horace do
Brink, Abram do
Brink, Jonas do
Brink, Wick do
Brink, David C. do
Brink, Mathew do
Brink, George do
Brink, Judson Coleville
Brink, Dewitt, do
Brink, John jr. do
Brink, Moses do
Brink, Janson do
Brink, Marcus do
Buchanan, J. H., Deckertown
Buchanan, Joseph do
Buchanan, W. H. do
Buchanan, J. Z. do
Buckley, Jas. do
Buckley, Amos do
Buckley, Simon W. do
Burcol, Christian, Coleville
Butler, John, Beemerville
Burns, Pat., Deckertown
Carr, G. R., Mt. Salem
Carr, Jas. G. do
Carr, John T. do
Carr, Asa, Deckertown
Carr, Geo. C. do
Carr, Thos. do
Casterline, D. C. do
Casterline, N., Union'lle, N. Y.
Casterline, N. D. do
Casterline, Geo. C. do
Casterline, W. B. do
Casterline, W. E. do
Cannon, F. M., Deckertown
Cannon, B. J. do
Carpenter, H. V., Coleville
Carpenter, M. C. do
Case, F. S., Deckertown
Caskey, Alva do
Caskey, John E. do
Caskey, W. A. do
Cassady, Wm. do
Cassady, Abe do
Cassady, Edwd. do
Carman, W. do
Christie, S., Unionville, N. Y.
Christie, Mahlon, Beemerville
Chardavoyne, H. H., Deck'wn
Chardavoyne, Gilbert, do
Clark, Isaiah, Mt. Salem

Clark, J. C., Mount Salem
Clark, J. H., do
Clark, J. H. jr., do
Clark, C. P. do
Clark, J. L. do
Clark, R. N., Deckertown
Clark, Warren, Beemerville
Clussman, H., Deckertown
Cole, George P. do
Cole, A. S. do
Cole, John P., Coleville
Cole, Eli do
Cole, W. V. do
Cole, John W. do
Cole, Josiah do
Cole, Henry do
Cole, Isaac do
Cole, H. J. do
Cole, John C. do
Cole, Martin do
Cole, P. H. do
Cole, J. C. do
Cole, Nelson do
Cole, W. jr. do
Cole, W. H., Deckertown
Cole, D. S. do
Compton, H. Coleville
Cox, W., Deckertown
Cox, W .W. do
Cox, J. M. do
Cox, L. J. do
Cox, James do
Cox, N. J. do
Cox, G. W., Coleville
Cox, W. jr., do
Cox, N. Unionville, N. Y.
Cox, J., Libertyville
Cooper, James, Deckertown
Cooper, C. E. do
Conklin, Thos., Deckertown
Conklin, James do
Conklin, Nicholas do
Conklin, J. W. do
Coykendall, J., Libertyville
Coykendall, M. do

Coykendall, M. D., Libertyville
Coykendall, D., do
Coykendall, S. do
Coykendall, L. H., Deckertown
Coykendall, G. do
Coykendall, Theo. do
Coykendall, Moses, Colville
Coykendall, E. S., Beemerville
Coe, W. T., Deckertown
Coe, George W. do
Cortright, Ira do
Cortright, B. do
Cortright, Jacob, Coleville
Cortright, H. do
Cortright, John do
Cortright, J. B. do
Cortright, Decker do
Cortright, Jackson do
Cortright, Enoch do
Cortright, E. B. do
Cortright, Peter do
Cortright, A. T. do
Cortright, James do
Cortright, Lewis do
Couse, J. H., Deckertown
Couse, Ben., Beemerville
Couse, Chas. B. do
Codington, Lynn do
Codington, Edw. do
Conway, Thos. do
Cosner, Lewis do
Corwin, Jesse, Coleville
Crisman, A., Unionville, N. Y.
Crane John N., Deckertown
Crane, A. G., do
Crane, B., Beemerville
Curran, J. D., Deckertown
Davie, C., Libertyville
Davenport, W. C. do
Davenport, H. P. do
Davenport, J. C. do
Davenport, Horace, Coleville
Davenport, Isaiah do
Davenport, L. C. do
Davenport, Eli do

Davenport, J. C. Coleville
Dewitt, Theo., do
Dewitt, Jacob, Unionville, N.Y.
Dewitt, Henry, Deckertown
Dewitt, Moses do
Dewitt, W. do
Dewitt, J. W. do
Dewitt, J. S. do
Dewitt, Evi do
Dewitt, Nelson do
Dewitt, B. M. do
Dewitt, J. E. do
Decker, A. J. do
Decker, John B. do
Decker, J. W. do
Decker, Fred. do
Decker, E A. do
Decker, W. L. do
Decker, Henry do
Decker, E. M. do
Decker, W. H. do
Decker, P. V. do
Decker, Jonathan do
Decker, P. P. do
Decker, Nelson do
Decker, L. R. do
Decker, M. do
Decker, James L. do
Decker, P. C. do
Decker, S. M. do
Decker, I. E. do
Decker, L. H. do
Decker, J. A. do
Decker, W. S. do
Decker, Isaac do
Decker, J. R. Mt. Salem
Decker, S. H. jr. do
Decker, T. H. do
Decker, Henry, Beemerville
Dennis, S., Deckertown
Dennis, J. A. do
Dennis, A. J. do
Dillison, Isaac do
Doty, H., Unionville, N. Y.
Doty, Ephraim do

Dolson, Isaac, Beemerville
Dotterer, J. B. Coleville
Dotterer, H. J. do
Durean, John, Deckertown
Dreer, Jacob do
Drake, Lewis do
Drake, Peter do
Drake, M. R., Libertyville
Dunn, O., Unionville, N. Y.
Dunn, T. J. do
Dunn, D. Deckertown
Dunn, L. J. do
Dunn, John H. do
Dunning, James do
Dunning, G. L., Beemerville
Dunning, J. H. do
Duril, W. E. Coleville
Dyrauf, Leonard, Deckertown
Eaton, Lewis, Beemerville
Eddy, D. A. Deckertown
Ellison, Walter do
Ellison, James do
Elston, C. do
Elston, J. W. do
Elston, Jos. W. do
Elston, Wm., Unionville, N. Y.
Elston, Asa do
Elston, J. C. do
Elston, M. W. do
Elston, Chas. W. do
Elston, Geo. T. do
Elston, W. jr., Mt. Salem
Emmans, A. Deckertown
Emmans, H. L. do
Everett, George, Coleville
Everett, D. B. do
Everett, Eliakim do
Everett, A. do
Everett, Thomas do
Everett, S. do
Everett, George jr. do
Everett, J. T. Deckertown
Fay, Frank, Coleville
Farley, J. E. do
Ferris, J. W. Deckertown

Fields, A. T., Deckertown
Fleming, John, do
Fleming, C. Unionville, N. Y.
Foster, David, Deckertown
Fountain, Thos. do
Fountain, E. C. do
Fountain, W. H. do
Fountain, John A. do
Fredericks, G. Unionville, N.Y.
Fuller, Theo. do
Fuller, Constant do
Fuller, Beach do
Fuller, M. W. do
Fuller, F. H. do
Fuller, J. P. do
Fuller, L. do
Fuller, W. C. Coleville
Fuller, Ely do
Garrison, Geo. do
Garrison, S. Deckertown
Gallagher, John do
Gall, D. H. Unionville, N Y
Georgia, L. M. Beemerville
Gibson, G. B. Coleville
Gibson, M. S. do
Gray, Thos., Deckertown
Groover, O. Unionville, N Y
Hall, Levi, Deckertown
Hall, Newman do
Hartwell, S. S. Unionville, N Y
Haggerty, J. Beemerville
Haggerty, J. jr. do
Haggerty, B. Unionville, N Y
Havens, B. D., Deckertown
Havens, S. S. do
Havens, Asa do
Havens, L. J. do
Havens, Gabe do
Havens, J. O. do
Havens, Zeph do
Havens, Barret do
Hankinson, St'phn Coleville
Harden, T. Unionville N Y
Harden, T. V., do
Harden, Miles, Deckertown

Hait, Benj., Deckertown
Hait, John, do
Halsted, W., do
Halsted, John, do
Harrison, W. T., do
Hewitt, Mahlon, do
Hewitt, Sam'l, do
Heater, N. W., do
Heater, F. L., do
Heater, D. B., do
Heater, Benj., do
Heater, T., Beemerville
Heater, James H., do
Heater, Henry, do
Herring, M., Coleville
Hoyt, Peter, Deckertown
Hoyt, D. C., do
Hoyt, J. R., Mount Salem,
Hoyt, A. B., do
Hockenbery, P. W., Deckert'n
Hockenbery, H., do
Hockenbery, Wm., do
Hockenbery, Meritt, do
Hockenbery, Seth, do
Hockenbery, E. Beemerville
Hockenbery, P. G., do
Hough, Sandf'd, Deckertown
Hough, S. (painter), do
Hough, Harrison, Coleville
Hough, Peter, do
Hough, J. B., do
Hough, J. A., do
Hoffman, Ira D., do
Hoffman, H. D., do
Hoffman, Anthony, Deckert'n
Howell, B. D., do
Howell, Alpheus, do
Howell, W. C., Beemerville
Howell, John, do
Howell, Mahlon, do
Horton, Jas. H., Deckertown
Horton, George W., do
Hornbeck, J. E., do
Hutchinson, J. T., do
Hulse, J. D., do

Jervis, W. H., Deckertown
Jervis, George, do
Jervis, Joseph, do
Johnson, Robert, do
Johnson, L. T., do
Johnson, W. H., do
Johnson, John, do
Johnson, W., Coleville
Ketchim, Levi, Deckertown
Kernick, W., do
Kilpatrick, J., do
Kinney, C. F., do
Kinney, J. E., do
Kinney, J. W., do
Kithcart, D., do
Knap, Edw'd, do
Kyte, J. W., do
Kyte, Thomas, do
Latier, M. B., do
Latier, Martin, Libertyville
Latier, Levi, Coleville
Latier, Chas., do
Latier, L. J., do
Latier, Isaac, do
Layton, Jerre, Deckertown
Lawrence, James, do
Lambert, C., Deckertown
Lambert, Wm. C., do
Laforger, T., Coleville
Lattimore, R., do
Lane, V. H., Deckertown
Lewis, Chas., do
Lewis, W. S., do
Lewis, John C., do
Lewis, E. L., Libertyville
Leach, L. W., Deckertown
Leach, H. A., do
Leport, A. J., do
Leport, J. B., do
Leonard, Thomas, Coleville
Leets, Smith, do
Little, O. J., Deckertown
Little, Howard, do
Longcor, Peter, do
Longcor, R. M., do
Longcor W. C., Deckertown
Longcor, J. L., do
Longcor, Anthony, do
Long, M. F., do
Loomis, John, do
Loomis, L. J., do
Love, G. F., do
Ludlem, J., do
Ludlem, Gabe, do
Mann, Wm., do
Mann, Jos., do
Mann, Wilson, do
Martin, Lebbens, do
Martin, Humphrey, do
Martin, H., Jr., do
Martin, J. B. Deckertown
Martin, J. F., do
Martin, R. R., do
Martin, Levi, do
Martin, W. F., do
Martin, Stephen, do
Marshall, Theo., do
Mackerley, John, do
Mackerley L., do
Mackerley, Henry, do
Mabee, Nicholas, do
Marshall, W., do
Marshall, Oscar, do
Marshall, Theo., do
Marvin, A. J., do
Maloney, T., Unionville, N. Y.
Meeker, Jeptha, do
Meeker, W. N., Deckertown
Meeker, John S., do
Mead, Harvey, Coleville
Mead, I. V., do
Meafoy, J. H., Unionville, N.Y.
Middaugh, Josiah, Beemerville
Middaugh, Dan'l, do
Morrow, D., Deckertown
Morrow, Sam'l, do
Moore, John, do
Morris, Albert, do
Mulverhill, T., do
Munson, John, do

Munson, Amos, Decketown
Munson, Augustus, do
Mullen, Theo., do
Myres, S. C., do
Myres, J. D., Beemerville
Myres, A. V., Unionville, N. Y.
McBride, Geo. do
McBride, Anson, do
McCord, R. H., Deckertown
McCoy, Sam'l, Beemerville
McCoy, J. W., Deckertown
McCoy, L. R. do
McCoy, S. F. R. do
McCoy, Rand do
McCoy, W. S. do
McCoy, Roy do
McCoy, E. D. do
McCoy, S. H. do
McCarter, Henry, do
McDaniels, John, Beemerville
McDownie, W., do
McDavit, J. S., Deckertown
McMickle, Jas. do
McMickle, John, do
McMickle, Robt., do
McMickle, Robt., Beemerville
McManus, D. D., Deckertown
McNish, E. W. do
McNish, Andrew do
McWilliam, J. do
Nearpass, Benj., Coleville
Newman, Sam'l, Deckertown
Newman, John do
Nicholas, W. H. do
Noble, C. M. do
Noble, A. C. do
Noble, W. H. do
Northrup, Thos., Mount Salem
Northrup, Jas. R., do
Northrup, Charles, do
O'Brien, Thos., Coleville
Odell, J. K., Deckertown
Orstrom, John, Coleville
Otter, Joseph do
Overton, G. S., Deckrtown

Palmer, Joseph, Deckertown
Paugh, Thomas, Coleville
Paugh, Benj. do
Paugh, Marshall do
Parcel, Sam'l, Deckertown
Parcel, R. D. do
Parcel, S. M. do
Patten, John, Mount Salem
Perry, Sam'l, Coleville
Perry, John, do
Perry, D., Deckertown
Pettit, Geo. do
Pellet, W., do
Pellet, O. do
Phillips, George, Beemerville
Phillips, J. B. do
Poppino, Jacob, Deckertown
Potts, E., Coleville
Potter, S. C., Deckertown
Potter, Jesse do
Potter, John D. do
Potter, Amzi do
Potter, J., Beemerville
Post, Horace V., Deckertown
Post, James do
Post, J. E. do
Polly, Brit do
Predmore, Elias do
Prinkle, P. J. do
Quick, Andrew do
Quick, J. L. do
Quick, J. A. do
Quick, J. W., do
Quick, George G. do
Quick, Alva do
Quick, W. B., Unionville, N. Y.
Rahley, D., Deckertown
Randolph, R. F. do
Reed, W. do
Rhodimer, J. T., Beemerville
Richards, O. B., Libertyville
Riggs, H. C., Coleville
Riggs, Elijah do
Roloson, S. N. do
Rolo ou, James, Beemerville

Roloson, J. V., Beemerville
Roloson, D. B. do
Roloson, Amzi J. do
Roloson, W. C. do
Roloson, Nathan, Deckertown
Roloson, J. do
Roloson, Isaiah do
Roy, I. do
Roy, Lynn do
Roy, Stephen do
Roy, Andrew do
Roe, J. D. do
Roe, James do
Rodimer, J. do
Roder, Frank, Coleville
Rogers, J. D. do
Rogers, C., Unionville, N. Y.
Rosenkrans, Dan'l, do
Russel, W. B. do
Russel, Pat'k, Libertyville
Rutan, S. R., Deckertown
Rutan, P. C., Libertyville
Rutan, J. H., Beemerville
Sanders, John, Deckertown
Sayre, Thomas do
Sayer, S. H. do
Sanford, M. do
Schoonover, L. D., Mt. Salem
Searles, H. G., Deckertown
Shafer, Finley do
Shelley, James do
Shelley, Ford do
Shelley, W. H do
Shaw, R. P. do
Shepherd, Jesse do
Shepherd, George do
Shepherd, Henry do
Shay, Eph'm, Libertyville
Shute, Albert, Unionville, N.Y.
Shute, Oscar do
Shorter, James, Deckertown
Shorter, Thomas do
Shorter, W. J. do
Shorter, Gabriel do
Shorter, Abram do
Shorter, David, Deckertown
Simmons, Brice, Beemerville
Simmons, C. do
Simonson, W. do
Simonson, H. F. do
Simonson, John do
Simonson, Edw'd do
Simonson, Fred'k, Deckertown
Simpson, Good. do
Simpson, E. T., do
Sipley, W. B., Beemerville
Silsbee, H. do
Sigler, J. C. do
Sisco, Jacob, Coleville
Slate, Jacob do
Slacker, John, Deckertewn
Smalley, James, Coleville
Smalley, C. J. do
Smith, M. C. do
Smith, Abram, Deckertown
Smith, J. P. do
Smith, Asa, Unionvllle, N. Y.
Smith, E. F. do
Smith, H. C. do
Smith, J. N. do
Smith, J. E. do
Smith, Ezra, do
Smith, David do
Snook, A. C., Coleville
Space, James, Deckertown
Space, Wm., do
Space, W. B., Beemerville
Sprague, W. H., Deckertown
Stormes, Fred'k do
Stormes, James do
Stormes, W. do
Stoll, Albert, Mount Salem
Stiles, E. A., Deckertown
Stiles, W. A. do
Struble, H. D. do
Struble, R. M. do
Struble, Elias do
Struble, James do
Struble, H., do
Stivers, Jacob, Beemerville

Stanaback, Z., Deckertown
Stanaback, C. do
Stoddard, Simeon do
Stewart, John, Libertyville
Still, J. W., Beemerville
Stout, J. E., do
Sutton, R. A., Deekertown
Swarts, J. J. do
Swarts, Wm. do
Swarts, Jacob, Deckertown
Swarts, Z. do
Swarts, John do
Swarts, M. W. do
Swarts, George do
Swarts, Mahlon do
Swarts, B. J. do
Swarts, Peter J. do
Swarts, C. A. do
Swarts, P. P., Coleville
Taylor, John do
Taylor, J. H. do
Taylor, W. E., Unionville, N.Y.
Thornton, J. C., Deckertown
Thompson, John, Coleville
Titsworth, W., Deckertown
Titsworth, W. A. do
Titsworth, A. do
Titsworth, W. W. do
Titsworth, Jacob do
Titsworth, W. S. do
Townsend, Good., Coleville
Townsend, W. do
Trainer, C., Deckertown
Tuttle, Robert do
Tuttle, James do
Tuttle, J. F. do
Tuttle, E. C. do
Tully, Andrew, Beemerville
Vail, J. G., Coleville
Vail, Sanford do
Vail, T. do
Vail, Charles, Unionville, N.Y.
Vail, H. G. do
Van Auken, Jos., Libertyville
Van Auken, M. D. do
Van Auken, Virgil, Deckert'n
Van Auken, U., Beemerville
Van Auken, J. T. do
Van Auken, J. D. do
Van Auken, Henry do
Van Auken, Jos. A. do
Van Druff, S. S., Deckertown
Van Druff, Evi, do
Van Druff, W. S. do
Van Gorder, J., Beemerville
Van Gorder, W., Libertyville
Van Gilder, G., Unionv'e, N. Y.
Valentine, Silas, Deckertown
Vaninwegin S., Mount Salem
Vaninwegin, M. do
Van Orden, D. B., Deckertown
Van Riper, Fred., Deckertown
Van Riper, Wm. do
Van Riper, Thos. do
Van Riper, Giles de
Van Sickle, J. V, Libertyville
Van Sickle, Wm. do
Van Sickle, G. W. do
Van Sickle, James do
Van Sickle, E. do
Van Sickle, Edw'd do
Van Sickle, C. do
Van Sickle, Cha's do
Van Sickle, D. B. do
Van Sickle, Elias do
Van Sickle, Jacob do
Van Sickle, B., Unionville, N.Y.
Van Sickle, W. do
Van Sickle, N. do
Van Sickle, W. Y. do
Van Sickle, J. B. do
Van Sickle, Andrew do
Van Sickle, H. V., Deckertown
Van Sickle, Geo. W. do
Van Sickle, M. do
Van Sickle, T., Coleville
Van Sickle, G. N. do
Qan Sickle, J. D. do
Van Sickle, D. do
Van Sickle, Sam'l do

Van Strader, Isaac, Deckert'n
Warner, E.D., Unionville, N.Y.
Watkins, Eph., Deckertown
Welsh, B., Unionville, N. Y.
West, Wm., Deckertown
Westbrook, A. D. do
Westbrook, B. P. do
Westfall, John A., do
Westfall, M. do
Westfall, C. J., Beemerville
Wells, Richard, Deckertown
Wells, P. D., do
Whitaker, Edw'd do
Whitaker, Lewis do
Whitaker, John A. do
Whitaker, J. J. "
Whitaker, Jacob "
White, J. F. "
Whorry, M. C., Mount Salem
White, Asa, Unionville, N. Y.
Wilson, Augustus, Deckertown
Wilson, Asa, do
Wilson, E. A. do
Wilson, Mark do
Wilson, A. do
Wilson, Martin do
Wilson, G. T. do
Wilson, S. do
Wilson, P. do
Wilson, A. J., do
Wilson, George O., do
Wilson, M. do
Wilson, M., jr. do
Wilson, Henry do
Wilson, I. L., do
Wilson, Jacob, Deckertown
Wilson, Chas. A. do
Wilson, Wm. do
Wilson, George E. do
Wilson, Nelson do
Wilson, A., Unionville, N. Y.
Wilson, Lebbens, do
Wilson, Edw'd do
Wilson, Asa W., Mt. Salem.
Wilson, L., Libertyville
Wilson, John, Coleville
Wickham, Sam'l do
Wickham, J. J. do
Wickham, L. V. do
Wickham, Wm. do
Wickham, D. D. do
Wickham, C. D., Deckertown
Wickham, G. do
Williams, John do
Williams, Henry do
Winters, A., Mount Salem
Winters, Isaac do
Winfield, Jacob, Coleville
Winfield, W. B., do
Wolfe, Sam'l C., Beemerville
Wood, James H., Mt. Salem
Wood, A. T., Coleville
Wood, A. P.,, Deckertown
Woodruff, N. T. do
Wright, John do
Wright, W. T. do
Wright, J. do
Wright, N. B. do
Wright, Gee., Coleville

BUSINESS DIRECTORY

OF

SUSSEX COUNTY.

ANDOVER.

Allen, S. C., carriage manufactory
Coursen, J. A, groceries and provisions
Cook, Corson, lumber and coal
Davison, C. S., marble cutter
Freeman & Ayres, general store
Howe, Freeman, tin
Johnson & Smith, drugs, groceries, &c.
McKain & Cross, cheese factory
McKinney, W., flour mill and distillery
Miller & Davison, physicians
Stackhouse, N. A., general store
Van Natten, Wm., hotel

BALESVILLE.

Bale, John, grist, saw and woolen mills
Curry, E. M., general store
Northrup, J. & B., turning mill

BEAVER RUN.

Jones, Caleb & Sons, foundry & dry goods

BEEMERVILLE.

Adrian & Longcoy, carriage manuf'y, blacksmith
Beemer, G. L., general store
Couse, B., tannery
Dalson, I., carriage manuf., blacksmith
Dunning, J. H., general store, saw mill
Hockenbery, Elias, hotel
Howell, W. C., harness maker
Roleson, J. V., cabinet maker
Still, J., grist mill
Westfall, W., blacksmith & wheelwright
Westfall, E. J, physician

BRANCHVILLE.

Barbier Leather Manufacturing Co.
Bowman Geo. J., hotel
Bray & Phillips, general store
Chamberlain M., grist and saw mill
Cole & Cartwright, blacksmiths
Cornell, J. H. & Bro., nursery
Compton, Thomas, variety store
Crisman, Virgil H., grist mill
Decker & Wyker, freighters
Dunning, E A., general store
Gessner, Edw'd, clothing
Gray, Wm., flour mill
Hanasy, J. G., tailor
Howell, J. P., cooper
McCoy, Jas., harness
Matterson & Everitt, book, stationery, boots, shoes, &c.
Morris & Sherred, hotel
Roe & Decker, general store
Roe & Smith, dry goods
Speicher, John, harness
Stivers & McDonald, general store
Utter, Jno. J., wagons
Vanduzer, G. A., hardware
Whitaker, H., hotel and bakery
Williamson, J. H., carpenter

COLEVILLE.

Carpenter, M. C., harness
Cole, J. C., miller and cheesebox manuf'y
Compton, H. miller
Davenport, H. wheelwright
Dotterer, J. B., general store
Dotterer, Henry, hotel
Perrine, W. H., miller
Post, J. E., blacksmith
Taylor, J. H., hotel
Vail, T., general store

DECKERTOWN.

Ayres & Westbrook, butchers
Beemer, J. E., hotel
Bedell, Andrew, saloon
Canon, F. M., drugs
Casterlin, D. C., harness
Chardovoine, G., hotel
Coe, G. W., foundry
Cooper, J. H., saw mill
Cox, W. W., general store
Coykendall & Little, clothing
Decker & Dyraff, shoe dealers
Decker & Titsworth, general store
Dewitt & Eddy, furniture
Elston, J. W., general store
Farmers' National Bank
Foster, D., undertaker
Hait, Benj., baker
Heater & Munson, wagon makers
Heater & Hewitt, blacksmiths
Horton, J. H., livery
Jervis, W H., blacksmith
Kluseman, H, barber
Wilson, C. A., lumber and coal
Martin, L. J., lawyer
McCoy, W. S. & Co., hardware
Meeker, W. M., jeweler
Noble, N. B, & Co., drugs
Sayer & Noble, printers
Sayre, T., Jeweler
Searles, H. G., stoves and tin
Shaw R. P., manuf'y rakes, cradles, &c.
Spear, Wm., shoe store.

FLATBROOKVILLE.

Decker, J. S., general store
Smith & Fuller, general store

FRANKLIN FURNACE.

Cronin & Grimes, grocery
Dennis, Jesse, hotel
Franklin Iron Co., store, &c., &c.
Munson, C. & D. D., general store

GLENWOOD.

Bloom, A., general store

HAMBURGH.

Allen & Myers, tinners
Beardslee & Brown, millers
Benjamin, N. E., hotel
Bird, Clarkson, cheese
Carpenter, Alex., hotel
Corner, Hiram, wheelwright
Edsall, R. E. & Co., general store
Edsall T. J., blacksmith
Everitt & Hendershot, lumber
Lane, D. R., drugs
Martin, N. B., hotel
Smith, Jas. K., hotel
Smith, W. S. & Bro., general store
Ward, F. M., millwright
Woods, Smith, blacksmith

HAINESVILLE.

Clark, John Y., hotel
Knight, W. C., general store
Lorey, A. C., general store
Stoll, J. M., general store

HUNTSVILLE.

Wilson, Lewis, general store

LAFAYETTE.

Armstrong, O. P., grist mill & distillery
Bagster, J. J., general store
Collver & Huston, grist, saw mill & foun'y
Coit, Sylvester, wheelwright
Davie, Peter B., wheelwright
Emmons, Wm., cooper
Fields, Obedial, blacksmith
Hopper, Dan'l., blacksmith
Larow, J. B., hotel
Morris, John D., grocery
Monroe, David, sash and blind factory
Pollison, Wm. M., wheelwright
Quick, Clark, blacksmith
Ross, W. I., attorney-at-law
Shuster, Jacob, blacksmith
Van Natten, John, hotel

LAYTONS.

Cole, J., general store
Down, R., blacksmith
Hoffman, J., cabinetmaker
Lattimore, D. B., hotel, wheelwright
Tuttle, B. L., general store
Warbass, D. R., miller

McAFEE'S VALLEY.

Hamilton, Geo. W., hotel
Simpson, Wm., Jr., general store
Wright, Wm., wagon

MIDDLEVILLE.

Andrew, O., general store
Butler, J., miller
Keen, J. W., miller

MONROE CORNERS.

Braistead, Edward, hotel
Braistead, E. G., general store
Inglis, James R., hotel
Mathews, Theo., miller
Minion, J. W, miller
Stickle, Lewis, blacksmith
Sutton, J. H., general store

MONTAGUE.

Cole, Martin & Son, general store
Coykendal, A. J., general store
Hornbeck, Jacob, grist mill
Shimer, Joseph, grist and saw mill
Westbrook, J. J., blacksmith
Whittaker. W., hotel

MOUNT SALEM.

Carl, James, general store
Casterline & Son, blacksmiths
Whittaker, Mrs., hotel

NEWTON.

Anderson, Daniel S., lawyer, Park Place
Anderson House, Vernon & Garrison, propr's, Spring street
Anderson, Joseph, Spring st
Anderson & Johnson, lawyers, Park place
Arvis, Charles, general agent of Sussex Railroad
Baker, C. E., fancy goods, Spring st
Bennett, M. B., grocer and confectioner, Spring st
Blanchard, A. H., carriage maker, Mill st
Bunnell, Thos. G., publisher of *New Jersey Herald*, Spring st
Burhard, Anthony, harness, Spring st
Cannon, Peter, variety store, Spring st
Case, Timothy, supt. of Sussex Railroad, Halstead st
Casterline, Wm. D., insurance agt. High st
Clark, Hiram C., auctioneer and insurance agent, Park place
Cochran House, Ward & Kelsey, prop'rs, Spring st
Coult, Van Blarcom & Cochran, lawyers, cor Park and High sts
Cramer, R. A. books, stationery, etc. Main st
Criger, G. W., insurance agent, Spring st
Crook & Kimball, marble cutters, Spring street
Daire, Amand, carriage painter, Moran st
Decker & Hardin, lumber dealers, Spring street.
Duncan, David L., physician, Trinity st
Dunning, G. B., druggist, Spring st

Durling House, D. M. Dickson, prop'r, cor Water and Mill sts
English, J. & J., blacksmiths Spring st
Fellows, A. F., druggist, Spring st
Fox, Wm., boot and shoemaker, Spring st
Frase, Geo., carpenter and builder, Water street
Garrison & Poole, dentists, Spring st
Gillman, Carl, barber. Spring st
Goldenberg, David, dry goods and notions, Spring st.
Goodman, R. F., publisher *Sussex Register*, High st
Gordon, John A., blacksmith, Spring st
Gottoche, Augustus, cigars and tobacco, Spring st
Graey, Francis, harness, Spring st
Hamilton, Robert, lawyer, Trinity st
Hanke, Lewis, barber, Spring st
Hasbrouck, J., physician, High st.
Havens, Jonathan, physician, High st
Heller, R. & Co., wholesale wines and liquors, Water st
Hemingway, John, ticket agent, at depot, Spring st.
Heycht, D., boot and shoemaker, Spring street
Hough Brothers, groceries, dry goods, Spring st. *See adv.* "Domestic Sewing Machine.)
Hough & Ackerson, meat market, High st
Hull, David R., dry goods, groceries, boots, shoes, &c., Spring st., *See Adv.*
Hull, Gershon, Jr., boots, shoes aad leather, Spring st
Johnson' Sam'l, dry goods and groceries, cor Spring and Main sts
Johnson & Pittinger, paint manufactory, Moran st
Juler, Geo., saloon, Water st
Kaisting, Henry. saloon, Spring st
Kays, Thomas, lawyer, Spring st
Kerr, David M., blacksmith, Moran st
Kimball, Edward, blacksmith, Water st
Laing, S. E., fancy goods, Spring st. *See Adv*, Buyers' Union
Lane, John W.. stoves and tinware, Spring st
Leary, Edmond O., saloon, cor Spring and Water sts
Leport, Geo. R., baker. Spring st
Leport, Wm. H., dry goods, spring st.
Lockwood. D. C. & Co., manufs. of agricultural implements, cor Moran and Spring sts
Losee Abram, fish, oysters, &c., Spring st
Losee, John B., baker and confectioner, Spring street
Margarum, T. F., dry goods and groceries, Spring street
Mirkert, Julius, meat market, Park place
Moore, E. C., coal dealer, Spring st
Merchants National Bank, organized 1865; capital, $100,000. Robt. Hamilton, pres.; J. L. Swayze, cash., Spring st
Miller, L. D., physician, Main st
Murry, Thomas, saloon, Spring st
Myers, Wallace, clothing and notions, Spring st
National Hotel, Jesse Ward, prop'r, Spring st near Depot
New Jersey Herald, weekly, T. G. Bunnell, editor and publisher, Spring st
Newman, J. S., dentist, Spring st
Parsons, N. P., blacksmith, cor Water Trinity sts
Perrine & Howell, lawyers, High st
Peoples Mutual Life Insurance Co., W. W. Woodward, pres.; W. E. Ross, sec., High st
Reeve, O. D., tailor, Spring st
Roe, Charles, surrogate, High st
Rorbach, Charles, P., watches and jewelry, High st
Rosenkrans, L. D., dry goods, boots, shoes and groceries, Spring st
Rosenkrans, Martin, lawyer, High st
Ross, William E., justice of the peace, High st
Rudd Henry J., music and musical instruments, Main st
Ryerson, Thos., physician, Halstead st
Sayre, David M., phpsician, Park place
Schafer, Abraham, leather and hides, Spring st
Schealer, Abraham, saloon, Spring st
Schafer, books, stationery, &c., Spring st
Shepherd, Levi, lawyer, Park st
Sheppard, R. A., dentist. Main st
Shiner, C. H. & Co., harness makers, Spring st
Shupe, Mahlon, saloon, Spring st near Depot
Simpson, 'Edwd I., grocer and varieties, Spring st
Snyder & Warbasse, dry goods, groceries, carpets, &c., Spring st
Smaly, John, blacksmith, Spring st
Smith, D. W., groceries, provisions, &c., Spring st
Smith, G. L., druggist, Main st
Smith, James, sash, door, blind & spoke manufactory, Spring st
Smith, James L., furniture, High st
Smith, F. M. & N., saloon, Spring st
Squinten, James, saloon, Spring st
Stewart, Benjamin, stoves and tinware, cor Spring and Moran sts.
Stewart, John T., justice, cor Main st and Park place
Stoll, John, watches and jewelry, Spring street
Stoll, Dunn & Co., dry goods, Spring st
Stuble, Ludwig, watches and jewelry, Spring st
Stuart J. R. & Co., druggists, Spring st
Sussex National Bank, capital, $200,000; David Thompson, president, Church st
Sussex Register (weekly), R. F. Goodman, editor and publisher, High st
Sutton, Lewis H., stoves and tinware Spring st
Taylor, Wm. E., blacksmith, Moran st
Thompson, David, lawyer, High st

Trusdell, Ladner, chair manufactory, Park place
Tuttle & Tully, merchant tailors and clothiers, Spring st
Vancampen B. & S. J., leather hides and findings, Water st
Wald, E. W., boot and shoemaker, Water street
Ward House, High st
Ward & Kalsey, Cochran House, Spring street
Williams, J. C., furniture dealer, Spring Street
Wilson, E. B., barber, Spring st
Woodruff, Dawson, lawyer, High st
Woodruff & Hawley, saloon, Spring st
Woodruff, Wm. W., hardware, agricultural instruments, seeds, &c., Main st
Woychinske, carriage and Wagon maker, Water st

OGDENSBURG.

Adams, Wm., wholesale liquors,
Batson & Lauterman, builders
Edsall, John, carriage maker
George, John. general store
Lauterman, Wm. G. & Bro., general store
Rodgers, Dr. T. R., druggist
Struble, Jacob, hotel
Steinglanze, Jacob, clothing
Underwood, Rufus, blacksmith

SPARTA.

Andress, T, H., Apothecary
Boss, C. V., general store
Bradbury, B. B , boots and shoes
Decker James L., grist and saw mill, and distillery
Earle, Wm., hotel
Elliott. Samuel, wheelwright
Fisher, George B., harness
Goble, I. jr., general store
Lantz, A. J., miller
Mabee, Martin, hotel
McCormick, Calvin, blacksmith
Potter, John A., general store
Ross, John, wheelwright
Sanford, Collins, grocer
Steadworthy, J. & J., blacksmiths
Stillwell, Daniel, general store
Titman Jas. B., miller
Turnbell, Jacob, blacksmith
White John L., cooper

STANHOPE.

Bissell, J., blacksmith
Budd, S. D., general store
Cottrell, C. J., tanner
Crossen & Wintermute, market
Doremus Bros., stores and tinware
Fichter, John, hotel
Hull, A., wheelwright
King, A. G., justice, fancy store
Knight, John M , hotel
Knight, J. M. & Son, general store
Laurence & King, general store
Mills, Geo., harness
McGlaughlin & Mills, painters
Neldon & Lampson, physicians
Rose, J. & Son, bakers
Stackhouse, Wm, H. & Son, genera store
Thorpe, Moses, cabinet maker
Todd, Wm. Mrs., groceries
Van Arsdale, J, S., drugs, &c.
Wills, A. S., general store

STILLWATER.

Garniss, Geo., general store
Hoff, A., grocery
Moore, C. V., physician
Youmans, Martin, miller

SNUFFTOWN.

Lewis, James M,, general store
Longstreet, Wm. S., general store
Temple, E, W,, general store
Wright, E. H. & Co , general store

SWARTSWOOD.

Lattermore, Geo., hotel
McDanolds. Hugh, general store
Staley, A. J., blacksmith

VERNON.

Blanchard, A:, tanner
Conklin, J. S., wagons
DeKay. T. S., hotel
Denton, R, S,, general store
Givens, J., general store
Keiser, Aaron, blacksmith
Williams, J., I., general store
Wood, S. T , books

WALLPACK CENTRE.

Roe, Jacob general store
Winans, Theo., blacksmith

WATERLOO.

Smith, S. T., & Bro., general store mill, &c.

The New York Weekly Witness.

ONE DOLLAR PER ANNUM.

This paper, of which the second volume will begin with the new year, contains FORTY-EIGHT COLUMNS filled with the choicest reading matter, arranged somewhat as follows :

1st—About twelve columns of editorials and other original articles, many of the latter by able writers. Among those who have already contributed articles to the Witness are the Rev. Dr. John Hall. Rev. Dr. Ormiston, Rev. Dr. Deems, and Rev. Dr. Taylor, of New York; Rev. Dr. McCosh, President of Princeton College ; General O. O. Howard, Washington ; Rev. Newman Hall, London ; Rev. Dr. Wilkes, Montreal, and several other gentlemen of note.

2d.—About twelve columns are filled with selections from the editorial articles of the great New York dailies (*Herald*, *Tribune*, *Times*, *World*), and from the leading weekly religious papers. The ablest writers of the day are thus made to contribute to the interest and value of the WITNESS.

3d.—About twelve columns are filled with tales and selections from American and British magazines, religious weeklies, &c., all instructive and interesting for the various members of the family, including the young

4th.—About twelve columns are filled with News, Reports of Meetings, (including the Fulton Street Daily Prayer Meetings,) Prices Current, and a few advertisements.

Pages could be filled with highly favorable notices of the press and letters received from subscribers, but all we ask is a trial, and to that end subscriptions of 25 cents will be received for a quarter of a year, or from now till the New Year.

The WITNESS contains, to say the least, as much and as valuable matter as the weeklies at $2 to $3, and it will be readily seen that at one dollar it can neither afford premiums nor pictures. It relies upon the recommendations of those who read it and requests the co-operation of Christians of all denominations to diffuse a cheap American newspaper throughout the Union.

The following is the platform copied from the prospectus of the NEW YORK DAILY WITNESS, when it was issued, on 1st June, 1871, which is equally applicable to the WEEKLY WITNESS :

THE PLATFORM.

The WITNESS will be on the same platform with regard to religion as the Evangelical Alliance and Young Men's Christian Association; with regard to temperance as the American Temperance Society ; with regard to human rights irrespective of color, as the American Missionary Association ; with respect to treatment of animals, as Mr. Bergh ; and it will regard political questions only from a Christian standpoint.

The DAILY WITNESS is $3 per annum.

All communications to be addressed to the undersigned, to whom all money orders are to be made payable.

JOHN DOUGALL,
Proprietor DAILY WITNESS,
162 Nassau Street, New York.

The WEEKLY WITNESS will be sent from 1st of September to 1st of January (four months), to new Subscribers, for 25 cents, remitted in advance, and the paper invariably stops when the subscriptionexpires, unless previously renewed.

ONLY $2 A YEAR.

"SUSSEX CO. INDEPENDENT,"

PUBLISHED WEEKLY,

BY

SAYER & NOBLE,

DECKERTOWN, N. J.

Particular pains is taken to furnish our readers with all the Latest News.

The circulation of the SUSSEX CO. INDEPENDENT is rapidly increasing, and is one of the best advertising mediums in northern New Jersey,

SUBSCRIPTIONS ONLY $2 A YEAR, PAYABLE IN ADVANCE.

of every kind executed with neatness and dispatch.

BLANKS AND PAMPHLET PRINTING A SPECIALTY.

GIVE US A FAIR TRIAL.

STATISTICS.---1872.

TOWNSHIPS.	Population 1870.	Acres Assessed.	Amount of Real and Personal Estate.	Polls.	State, School, and County Tax.
Andover	1,126	13,000	$1,128,800	255	$4,577 00
Byram	1,332	18,895	1,037,720	312	4,510 00
Frankford	1,776	19,469	1 706,528	420	6,264 00
Green	868	12,650	1,229,563	201	4,756 00
Hampton	1,023	12,900	1,209 928	214	4,724 00
Hardyston	1,669	16,615	1,342,115	462	5,248 50
Lafayette	884	11,153	1,102,539	209	3,828 00
Montague	932	25,100	455,855	210	2,356 00
Newton	2,403	1,200	2,813,700	490	10,949 00
Sandyston	1,230	25 750	949 746	280	3,095 00
Sparta	2,031	24,029	1,732,666	479	7,101 00
Stillwater	1,632	21,735	1,160,827	357	4,811 00
Vernon	1,979	36,150	949,746	405	5,814 00
Wallpack	647	11,500	544,697	148	2,018 50
Wantage	3 636	41,050	3,406,830	800	13,669 00
Total	23,168	291,196	$20,831,280	5 243	$83 721 00

STATE OFFICERS, JUDGES, Etc.--1872.

Governor.—Hon. Joel Parker, Jr,

Secretary of State.—Hon. Henry C. Kelsey.

Treasurer.—Hon. Josephus Sooy, Jr.

Comptroller.—Hon. Albert L. Runyon.

Attorney General.—Robert Gilchrist.

Governor's Private Secretary.—John A Hall.

Clerk in Chancery.—Henry S. Little.

Clerk of the Supreme Court.—Charles P. Smith.

Major General.—Theodore Runyon.

Quartermaster General.—Lewis Perrine.

Adjutant General.—William S. Stryker.

Inspector General.—J. Augustus Fay, Jr.

Asst. Adj. General.—S. Meredith Dickinson.

State Department—J. D. Hall.

Comptroller Department.—E. J. Anderson.

Treasury Department.—W. Budd Deacan.

Chief Clerk Sopreme Court.—Alfred Lawshe.

Chancellor.- Hon. Abraham O. Zabriskie.

Vice Chancellor.—Hon. Amzi Dodd.

Chief Justice.—Hon. Mercer Bearsley,

Justices Supreme Court.—Hon. Joseph D. Bedle, Hon. V. Dalrimple, Hon. Geo. S. Woodhull, Hon. Edward W. Scudder, Hon. Bennet Van Syckle, Hon. David A. Depue.

Judges Court of Errors.—Hon. Azi Dodd, Hon. E. L. B, Wales, Hon. John Clement, Hon. Francis S. Lathrop, Hon. James L. Ogden, Hon. Chas. S. Olden.

State Librarian—James S. McDanolds.

State Supt. Public Schools.—E. A. Apgar.

Principal State Normal School.—Louis M. Johnson.

Keeper of the State Prison.—Robert H. Howell.

Supervisor State Prison.—William R. Murphy.

State Geologist.—Geo. H. Cook.

Secretary of the Senate.—John F. Babcock.

Clerk of the House.—Sinickson Chew.

THE LEGISLATURE.

FROM SUSSEX COUNTY.

Senate.—Richard E. Edsall. *Assembly.*—Lebbeus Martin.

INDEX

www.ingramcontent.com/pod-product-compliance
Lightning Source LLC
Chambersburg PA
CBHW060800110426
42739CB00032BA/2303

9781556136726